Take a Chance

BRITANNICA
Mathematics
in
Context

Data Analysis and Probability

TEACHER'S GUIDE

HOLT, RINEHART AND WINSTON

Mathematics in Context is a comprehensive curriculum for the middle grades. It was developed in 1991 through 1997 in collaboration with the Wisconsin Center for Education Research, School of Education, University of Wisconsin-Madison and the Freudenthal Institute at the University of Utrecht, The Netherlands, with the support of the National Science Foundation Grant No. 9054928.

The revision of the curriculum was carried out in 2003 through 2005, with the support of the National Science Foundation Grant No. ESI 0137414.

National Science Foundation

Opinions expressed are those of the authors and not necessarily those of the Foundation.

Jonker, V., van Galen, F., Boswinkel, N., Wijers, M., Bakker, A., Simon, A. N., Burrill, G., & Middleton, J. A. (2005). *Take a chance*. In Wisconsin Center for Education Research & Freudenthal Institute (Eds.), Mathematics in Context. Chicago: Encyclopædia Britannica.

The Teacher's Guide for this unit was prepared by David C. Webb, Teri Hedges, Truus Dekker & Monica Wijers.

ISBN 0-03-039802-9

1 2 3 4 5 6   073   09 08 07 06 05

The *Mathematics in Context* Development Team

Development 1991–1997

The initial version of *Take a Chance* was developed by Vincent Jonker, Frans van Galen, Nina Boswinkel, and Monica Wijers. It was adapted for use in American schools by Aaron N. Simon, Gail Burrill, and James A. Middleton.

Wisconsin Center for Education

Research Staff

Thomas A. Romberg
Director

Joan Daniels Pedro
Assistant to the Director

Gail Burrill
Coordinator

Margaret R. Meyer
Coordinator

Project Staff

Jonathan Brendefur
Laura Brinker
James Browne
Jack Burrill
Rose Byrd
Peter Christiansen
Barbara Clarke
Doug Clarke
Beth R. Cole
Fae Dremock
Mary Ann Fix

Sherian Foster
James A, Middleton
Jasmina Milinkovic
Margaret A. Pligge
Mary C. Shafer
Julia A. Shew
Aaron N. Simon
Marvin Smith
Stephanie Z. Smith
Mary S. Spence

Freudenthal Institute Staff

Jan de Lange
Director

Els Feijs
Coordinator

Martin van Reeuwijk
Coordinator

Mieke Abels
Nina Boswinkel
Frans van Galen
Koeno Gravemeijer
Marja van den Heuvel-Panhuizen
Jan Auke de Jong
Vincent Jonker
Ronald Keijzer
Martin Kindt

Jansie Niehaus
Nanda Querelle
Anton Roodhardt
Leen Streefland

Adri Treffers
Monica Wijers
Astrid de Wild

Revision 2003–2005

The revised version of *Take a Chance* was developed by Arthur Bakker and Monica Wijers. It was adapted for use in American schools by Gail Burrill.

Wisconsin Center for Education

Research Staff

Thomas A. Romberg
Director

David Webb
Coordinator

Gail Burrill
Editorial Coordinator

Margaret A. Pligge
Editorial Coordinator

Freudenthal Institute Staff

Jan de Lange
Director

Truus Dekker
Coordinator

Project Staff

Beth R. Cole
Erin Hazlett
Teri Hedges
Carrie Johnson
Jean Krusi
Elaine McGrath
Margaret R. Meyer

Anne Park
Bryna Rappaport
Kathleen A. Steele
Anna C. Stephens
Candice Ulmer
Jill Vettrus

Mieke Abels
Arthur Bakker
Peter Boon
Els Feijs
Dédé de Haan
Martin Kindt

Nathalie Kuijpers
Huub Nilwik
Sonia Palha
Martin van Reeuwijk
Monica Wijers

Cover photo credits: (left, right) © Getty Images; (middle) © Corbis

Illustrations
4 (bottom) Jason Millet; **6** (top left and right) Mona Daily;
(bottom) Jason Millet; **13** (top, bottom left, and middle), **15** (top
and bottom) Jason Millet; **23, 23T** (top) Holly Cooper-Olds; (bottom left)
Mona Daily; **27** (all) **31** (left) Jason Millet

Photographs
1B © PhotoDisc/Getty Images; **1**(all) Mary Stone Photography/HRW;
2, 3 (left) Victoria Smith/HRW; (middle) Mary Stone Photography/HRW;
(right) © PhotoDisc/Getty Images; **7** (top left) © PhotoDisc/Getty
Images; (top right) Mary Stone Photography/HRW; (bottom) John
Langford/HRW; **23, 26, 26T** © PhotoDisc/ Getty Images; **27** (all) Mary
Stone/HRW; **29** (top) Mary Stone/HRW; (bottom) Peter Van Steen/HRW
Photo; **30** Peter Van Steen/HRW Photo

Contents

Letter to the Teacher   vi

Overview

NCTM Principles and Standards
  for School Mathematics   vii
Math in the Unit   viii
Data Analysis and Probability Strand:
  An Overview   x
Student Assessment in MiC   xiv
Goals and Assessment   xvi
Materials Preparation   xviii

Student Materials and Teaching Notes

Student Book Table of Contents
Letter to the Student

Section A   Fair

Section Overview   1A
Hillary and Robert   1
Choosing   2
Fair Again   3
Making a Spinner   4
Different Chance Objects   6
The Concert   6
Summary   8
Check Your Work   8

Section B   What's the Chance?

Section Overview   10A
Up and Down Events   10
Match 'Em Up   12
Frog Newton   13
Spinners   16
Summary   18
Check Your Work   18

Section C   Let the Good Times Roll

Section Overview   20A
Chancy Business   20
Now We're Rolling!   21
Tossing and Turning   22
Think B4 You Act   23
Find the Chance   23
Summary   24
Check Your Work   24

Section D   Let Me Count the Ways

Section Overview   26A
Families   26
Robert's Clothes   27
Hillary's Clothes   27
Two Children Again   28
Open or Closed?   29
Sum It Up   29
Treasure   31
Summary   32
Check Your Work   32

Additional Practice   34

Assessment and Solutions

Assessment Overview   40
Quiz 1   42
Quiz 2   44
Unit Test   46
Quiz 1 Solutions   48
Quiz 2 Solutions   49
Unit Test Solutions   50

Glossary

Take a Chance Glossary   52

Blackline Masters

Letter to the Family   54
Student Activity Sheets   55

Dear Teacher,

Welcome! *Mathematics in Context* is designed to reflect the National Council of Teachers of Mathematics *Principles and Standards for School Mathematics* and the results of decades of classroom-based educational research. *Mathematics in Context* was designed according to the principles of Realistic Mathematics Education, a Dutch approach to mathematics teaching and learning. In this approach mathematical content is grounded in a variety of realistic contexts in order to promote student engagement and understanding of mathematics. The term *realistic* is meant to convey the idea that contexts and mathematics can be made "real in your mind." Rather than relying on you to explain and demonstrate generalized definitions, rules, or algorithms, students investigate questions directly related to a particular context and develop mathematical understanding and meaning from that context.

The curriculum encompasses nine units per grade level. This unit is designed to be the second in the Data Analysis and Probability strand for Grade 6, but it also lends itself to independent use—to introduce students to elementary notions of probability using spinners, number cubes, and other tools that can represent chance situations.

In addition to the Teacher's Guides and Student Books, *Mathematics in Context* offers the following components that will inform and support your teaching:

- *Teacher Implementation Guide,* which provides an overview of the complete system and resources for program implementation;
- *Number Tools and Algebra Tools,* which are black-line master resources that serve as review sheets or practice pages to support the development of basic skills and extend student understanding of concepts developed in number and algebra units;
- *Mathematics in Context Online,* which is a rich, balanced resource for teachers, students, and parents looking for additional information, activities, tools, and support to further students' mathematical understanding and achievements.

Thank you for choosing *Mathematics in Context.* We wish you success and inspiration!

Sincerely,

The Mathematics in Context Development Team

Take a Chance
and the NCTM Principles and Standards for School Mathematics for Grades 6–8

The process standards of Problem Solving, Reasoning and Proof, Communication, Connections, and Representation are addressed across all *Mathematics in Context* units.

In addition, this unit specifically addresses the following PSSM content standards and expectations:

Number and Operations

In grades 6–8 all students should:

- compare and order fractions and percents efficiently and find their approximate locations on a number line and
- understand and use ratios to represent quantitative relationships.

Data Analysis and Probability

In grades 6–8 all students should:

- understand and use appropriate terminology to describe complementary and mutually exclusive events;
- use proportionality and a basic understanding of probability to make and test conjectures about the results of experiments and simulations; and
- compute probabilities for simple compound events, using such methods as organized lists, tree diagrams, and area models.

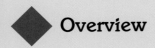

Math in the Unit

Prior Knowledge

This unit assumes that students can use simple percents and fractions to describe situations when appropriate and that they can order simple percents and fractions.

They must be able to connect simple ratios to fractions and percents.

Students should have an informal understanding of the mean. In addition, it may be helpful if students have familiarity with coins, number cubes, and spinners.

Facility with adding and subtracting up to three-digit numbers and multiplying and dividing two-digit numbers is helpful for this unit. Students should also have some knowledge about reading tables and using a number line to represent and order numbers.

Take a Chance is the second unit in the Data Analysis and Probability strand. Beginning with the concept of fairness, the unit progresses naturally to everyday situations involving chance and probability. Students analyze games and other situations where fairness is important.

Many of the problems are set in the fictional context of the daily life of two students, Hillary and Robert. These students consider how and whether such tools as number cubes, spinners, or coins can be used in a particular situation to make a fair decision.

A numerical value for the probability that an event occurs is introduced using a scale known as a *chance ladder*. Students order different events on this scale according to the probability each event will occur. They select a point on the scale to represent the chance of an event. First, the probability scale is informal: ranging from "sure it won't happen," "not sure," to "sure it will happen." Later the probability scale is formalized and ranges from 0% to 100% in steps of 10%.

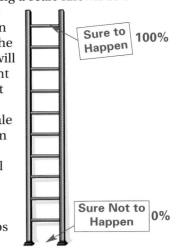

Chances are also expressed in proportional notation such as "1 out of 4." This notation is connected to simple fractions; 1 out of 4 is the same as $\frac{1}{4}$. These are related to percents by using the chance scale.

At first, chances are only estimated. Most questions focus on "Is this fair?" "How many possible outcomes exist?" "How many of these are favorable?" "Which is the more likely outcome?" Later in the unit, students calculate chances and express them as ratios, fractions, or percents. This is done for experimental chances (for example, results of tossing an item 30 times), and for theoretical chances (for example, the possible sums when rolling two number cubes).

Students identify combinations and possible outcomes of multiple-event situations, using tree diagrams and tables. The tree diagram is used as a model to count all possible outcomes. Later the tree diagram is also used to find favorable outcomes in different situations by tracing the paths in the tree diagram. The tree diagram is used in situations with two or three combined events.

When students have finished the unit they:

• understand the meaning of *fair* and how it relates to chance;

• know how to use tools for making fair decisions;

• understand the meaning of *chance* or *probability*; (They understand this at a preformal level. A formal definition of chance is introduced in the unit *A Second Chance*.)

• can estimate and order chances; (They do this on a preformal level, and on a more formal level in simple situations where they can easily calculate the chances.)

• use repeated trials to estimate chance (experimental chance);

• can determine all combinations and possible outcomes using tree diagrams and tables;

• can use visual models to estimate and calculate chance; (The models used are: chance ladders, chance scales, tree diagrams, and tables. Computing chance is usually done by "counting" in situations with few outcomes. This results in the chance expressed as "so many out of so many." Calculating chance in more complex situations using a definition is done in the unit *A Second Chance*. In that unit the tree diagram is formalized into a chance tree.)

• express chance for simple and multiple-event situations using percents, fractions, and ratios;

• compare theoretical and experimental probability. (They do this on a preformal level. In the unit *A Second Chance,* this is elaborated and formalized.)

Hillary	Robert	Kevin	Winner
			Robert
			Hillary
			No Winner

The Data Analysis and Probability Strand: An Overview

One thing is for sure: our lives are full of uncertainty. We are not certain what the weather will be tomorrow or which team will win a game or how accurate a pulse rate really is. Data analysis and probability are ways to help us measure variability and uncertainty. A central feature of both data analysis and probability is that these disciplines help us make numerical conjectures about important questions.

The techniques and tools of data analysis and probability allow us to understand general patterns for a set of outcomes from a given situation such as tossing a coin, but it is important to remember that a given outcome is only part of the larger pattern. Many students initially tend to think of individual cases and events, but gradually they learn to think of all features of data sets and of probabilities as proportions in the long run.

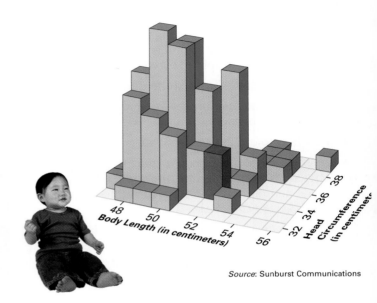

Source: Sunburst Communications

The MiC Approach to Data Analysis and Probability

The Data Analysis and Probability units in MiC emphasize dealing with data, developing an understanding of chance and probability, using probability in situations connected to data analysis, and developing critical thinking skills.

 The strand begins with students' intuitive understanding of the data analysis concepts of *most*, *least*, and *middle* in relation to different types of *graphical representations* that show *the distribution of data* and the probability concepts of *fairness* and *chance*. As students gradually formalize these ideas, they use a variety of counting strategies and graphical representations. In the culminating units of this strand, they use formal rules and strategies for calculating probabilities and finding measures of central tendency and spread.

Throughout this development, there is a constant emphasis on interpreting conclusions made by students and suggested in the media or other sources. In order for students to make informed decisions, they must understand how information is collected, represented, and summarized, and they examine conjectures made from the information based on this understanding. They learn about all phases of an investigative cycle, starting with questions, collecting data, analyzing them, and communicating about the conclusions. They are introduced to inference by sampling to collect data and reflect on possible sources of bias. They develop notions of random sampling, variation and central tendency, correlation, and regression. Students create, interpret, and reflect on a wide range of graphical representations of data and relate these representations to numerical summaries such as mean, mode, and range.

Organization of the Strand

Statistical reasoning based on data is addressed in all data analysis and probability units. Students' work in these units is organized into two substrands: data analysis and chance. As illustrated in the following map of the strand, the three core units that focus on data analysis are *Picturing Numbers*, *Dealing with Data*, and *Insights into Data*. The two units that focus on probability are *Take a Chance* and *A Second Chance*. The sixth core unit in this strand, *Great Predictions*, integrates data analysis and probability.

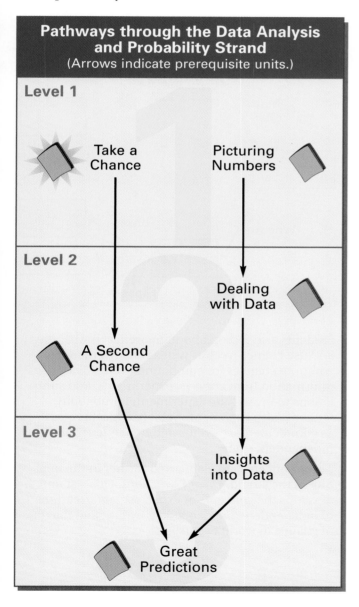

Data Analysis

In the units of the data analysis sub-strand, students collect, depict, describe, and analyze data. Using the statistical tools they develop, they make inferences and draw conclusions based on data sets.

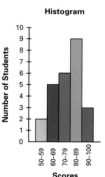

The substrand begins with *Picturing Numbers*. Students collect data and display them in tabular and graphical forms, such as histograms, number line plots, and pie charts. Measures of central tendency, such as the mean, are used informally as students interpret data and make conjectures.

In *Dealing with Data*, students create and interpret scatter plots, box plots, and stem-and-leaf plots, in addition to other graphical representations. The mean, median, mode, range, and quartiles are used to summarize data sets. Students investigate data sets with outliers and make conclusions about the appropriate use of the mean and median.

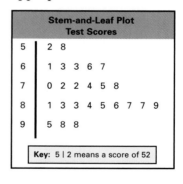

Sampling is addressed across this substrand, but in particular in *Insights into Data*, starting with informal notions of representative samples, randomness, and bias. Students gather data using various sampling techniques and investigate the differences between a survey and a sample. They create a simulation to answer questions about a situation. Students also consider how graphical information can be misleading, and they are introduced informally to the concepts of regression and correlation.

In *Great Predictions*, students learn to recognize the variability in random samples and deepen their understanding of the key statistical concepts of randomness, sample size, and bias. As the capstone unit to the Data Analysis and Probability strand, data and chance concepts and techniques are integrated and used to inform conclusions about data.

Chance

Beginning with the concept of fairness, *Take a Chance* progresses to everyday situations involving chance. Students use coins and number cubes to conduct repeated trials of an experiment. A chance ladder is used as a model throughout the unit to represent the range from impossible to certain and ground the measure of chance as a number between 0 and 1. Students also use tree diagrams to organize and count, and use benchmark fractions, ratios, and percents to describe the probability of various outcomes and combinations.

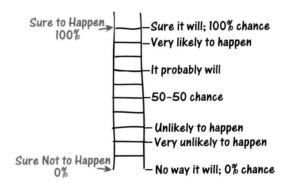

The second probability unit, *A Second Chance,* further develops students understanding of fairness and the quantification of chance. Students make chance statements from data presented in two-way tables and in graphs.

	Men	Women	Total
Glasses	32	3	35
No Glasses	56	39	95
Total	88	42	130

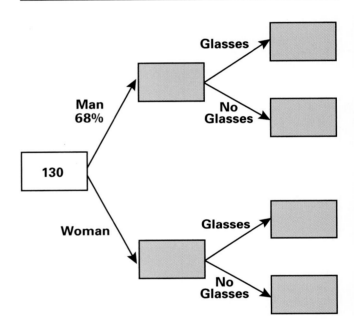

Students also reason about theoretical probability and use chance trees as well as an area model to compute chances for compound events. They use information from surveys, experiments, and simulations to investigate experimental probability. Students also explore probability concepts such as complementary events and dependent and independent events.

These concepts are elaborated further in the final unit of the strand, *Great Predictions.* This last unit develops the concepts of expected value, features of independent and dependent events, and the role of chance in world events.

Critical Reasoning

Critical reasoning about data and chance is a theme that exists in every unit of the Data Analysis and Probability strand. In *Picturing Numbers*, students informally consider factors that influence data collection, such as the wording of questions on a survey, and they compare different graphs of the same data set. They also use statistical data to build arguments for or against environmental policies.

In *Take a Chance*, students use their informal knowledge of fairness and equal chances as they evaluate decision-making strategies.

In *Dealing with Data*, students explore how the graphical representation of a data set influences the conjectures and conclusions that are suggested by the data. They compare advantages and disadvantages of various graphs and explore what you learn from using different measures of central tendency.

Throughout the curriculum, students are asked to view representations critically. Developing a critical attitude is especially promoted in *Insights into Data*, when students analyze graphs from mass media.

In *A Second Chance*, students explore the notion of dependency (for instance, the relation of gender and wearing glasses) and analyze statements about probabilities (for instance about guessing during a test).

In *Great Predictions*, students study unusual samples to decide whether they occurred by chance or for some other reason (pollution, for instance). They explore how expected values and probability can help them make decisions and when this information could be misleading.

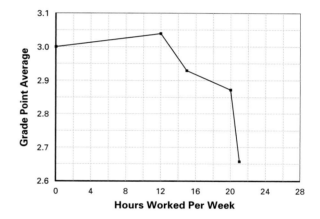

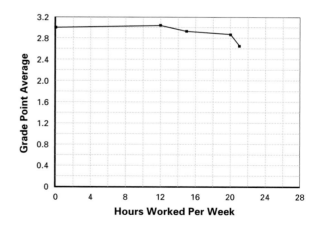

Student Assessment in Mathematics in Context

As recommended by the NCTM *Principles and Standards for School Mathematics* and research on student learning, classroom assessment should be based on evidence drawn from several sources. An assessment plan for a *Mathematics in Context* unit may draw from the following overlapping sources:

- **observation—As students work individually or in groups, watch for evidence of their understanding of the mathematics.**

- **interactive responses—Listen closely to how students respond to your questions and to the responses of other students.**

- **products—Look for clarity and quality of thought in students' solutions to problems completed in class, homework, extensions, projects, quizzes, and tests.**

Assessment Pyramid

When designing a comprehensive assessment program, the assessment tasks used should be distributed across the following three dimensions: mathematics content, levels of reasoning, and difficulty level. The Assessment Pyramid, based on Jan de Lange's theory of assessment, is a model used to suggest how items should be distributed across these three dimensions. Over time, assessment questions should "fill" the pyramid.

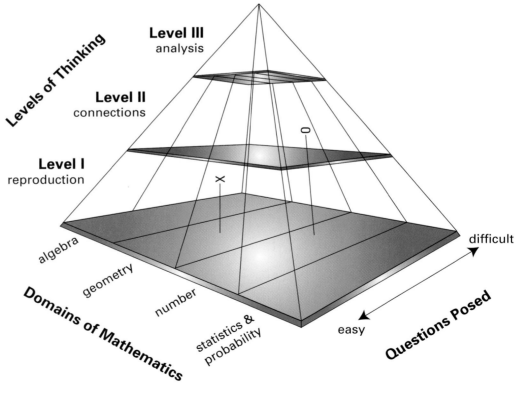

Levels of Reasoning

Level I questions typically address:

- recall of facts and definitions and
- use of technical skills, tools, and standard algorithms.

As shown in the pyramid, Level I questions are not necessarily easy. For example, Level I questions may involve complicated computation problems. In general, Level I questions assess basic knowledge and procedures that may have been emphasized during instruction. The format for this type of question is usually short answer, fill-in, or multiple choice. On a quiz or test, Level I questions closely resemble questions that are regularly found in a given unit, substituted with different numbers and/or contexts.

Level II questions require students to:

- integrate information;
- decide which mathematical models or tools to use for a given situation; and
- solve unfamiliar problems in a context, based on the mathematical content of the unit.

Level II questions are typically written to elicit short or extended responses. Students choose their own strategies, use a variety of mathematical models, and explain how they solved a problem.

Level III questions require students to:

- make their own assumptions to solve open-ended problems;
- analyze, interpret, synthesize, reflect; and
- develop one's own strategies or mathematical models.

Level III questions are always open-ended problems. Often, more than one answer is possible, and there is a wide variation in reasoning and explanations. There are limitations to the type of Level III problems that students can be reasonably expected to respond to on time-restricted tests.

The instructional decisions a teacher makes as he or she progresses through a unit may influence the level of reasoning required to solve problems. If a method of problem solving required to solve a Level III problem is repeatedly emphasized during instruction, the level of reasoning required to solve a Level II or III problem may be reduced to recall knowledge, or Level I reasoning. A student who does not master a specific algorithm during a unit but solves a problem correctly using his or her own invented strategy may demonstrate higher-level reasoning than a student who memorizes and applies an algorithm.

The "volume" represented by each level of the Assessment Pyramid serves as a guideline for the distribution of problems and use of score points over the three reasoning levels.

These assessment design principles are used throughout *Mathematics in Context.* The Goals and Assessment charts that highlight ongoing assessment opportunities — on pages xvi and xvii of each Teacher's Guide — are organized according to levels of reasoning.

In the Lesson Notes section of the Teacher's Guide, ongoing assessment opportunities are also noted by the Assessment Pyramid icon, located in the bottom left corner of each page of the Teacher's Guide.

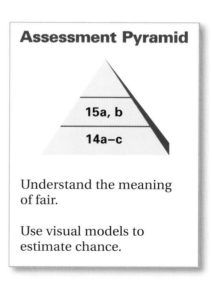

Assessment Pyramid

15a, b

14a–c

Understand the meaning of fair.

Use visual models to estimate chance.

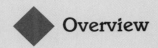
Goals and Assessment

In the *Mathematics in Context* curriculum, unit goals organized according to levels of reasoning described in the Assessment Pyramid on page xiv, relate to the strand goals and the NCTM *Principles and Standards for School Mathematics*. The *Mathematics in Context* curriculum is designed to help students demonstrate their under-

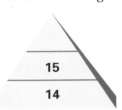

standing of mathematics in each of the categories listed below. Ongoing assessment opportunities are also indicated on their respective pages throughout the Teacher's Guide by an Assessment Pyramid icon.

It is important to note that the attainment of goals in one category is not a prerequisite to the attainment of those in another category. In fact, students should progress simultaneously toward several goals in different categories. The Goals and Assessment table is designed to support preparation of an assessment plan.

	Goal	Ongoing Assessment Opportunities	End-of-Unit Assessment Opportunities
Level I: Conceptual and Procedural Knowledge	**1.** Understand the meaning of fair and how it relates to chance.	**Section A** p. 5, #16, #17 p. 7, #21a-d **Section B** p. 16, #14a-c	**Quiz 1** #1a **Test** #1, #8
	2. Know how to use tools for making fair decisions.	**Section A** p. 9, For Further Reflection **Section B** p. 16, #14a-c	**Quiz 1** #1b, #2ab **Quiz 2** #4b **Test** #3
	3. Estimate and order chance events.	**Section B** p. 11, #4 p. 12, #5	**Quiz 1** #3abc, #4 **Test** #4, #5
	4. Express chance in percents, fractions, or ratios.	**Section B** p. 14, #11a-d **Section C** p. 23, #14	**Quiz 1** #3abc, #4 **Quiz 2** #1a, #4a **Test** #2, #4, #7ac
	5. List the possible outcomes of simple chance and counting situations.	**Section D** p. 29, #13	**Quiz 2** #2, #3bc **Test** #1

	Goal	Ongoing Assessment Opportunities	End-of-Unit Assessment Opportunities
Level II: Reasoning, Communicating, Thinking, and Making Connections	**6.** Understand the meaning of chance or probability.	**Section C** p. 25, For Further Reflection	**Quiz 2** #1b **Test** #6
	7. Use repeated trails to estimate chance.	**Section D** p. 26, #2	
	8. Use visual models to represent simple one-, two-, and three-event situations.	**Section B** p. 16, #15ab **Section D** p. 30, #20a-c	**Quiz 2** #2, #3abcd

	Goal	Ongoing Assessment Opportunities	End-of-Unit Assessment Opportunities
Level III: Modeling, Generalizing, and Non-Routine Problem Solving	**9.** Understand that variability is inherent in any probability situation.	**Section C** p. 21, #7	**Quiz 2** #1b **Test** #7b, #8
	10. Model real-life situations involving probability.	**Section D** p. 31, #25	
	11. Compare theoretical and experimental probability.	**Section B** p. 15, #13 **Section C** p. 25, For Further Reflection	

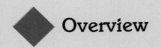
Materials Preparation

The following items are the necessary materials and resources to be used by the teacher and students throughout the unit. For further details, see the Section Overviews and the Materials part of the Hints and Comments section at the top of each teacher page. Note: Some contexts and problems can be enhanced through the use of optional materials. These optional materials are listed in the corresponding Hints and Comments section.

Student Resources

Quantities listed are per student.

- **Letter to the Family**
- **Student Activity Sheets 1–4**

Teacher Resources

Quantities listed are per class.

- **Board eraser**
- **Copy of spinner (student page 6)**
- **Small paper cup**
- **Bottle cap**
- **Large paper cup**

Student Materials

Quantities listed are per pair of students, unless otherwise noted.

- **Black crayon (one per student)**
- **Brad**
- **Coin**
- **Compass**
- **Different colored number cubes, two**
- **Drawing paper (seven sheets per student)**
- **Newspaper**
- **Paper clip**
- **Pennies, two**
- **Protractor**
- **Ruler**
- **Six-sided pencil**
- **Spinners**
- **Tacks, two**

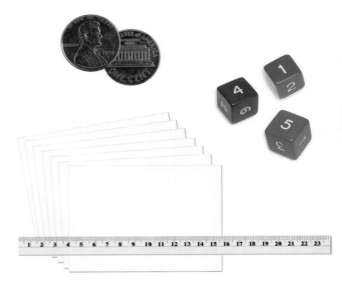

BRITANNICA
Mathematics in Context

Student Material and Teaching Notes

◆ **Contents**

Letter to the Student   vi

Section **A**   **Fair**

    Hillary and Robert   1
    Choosing   2
    Fair Again   3
    Making a Spinner   4
    Different Chance Objects   6
    The Concert   6
    Summary   8
    Check Your Work   8

Section **B**   **What's the Chance?**

    Up and Down Events   10
    Match 'Em Up   12
    Frog Newton   13
    Spinners   16
    Summary   18
    Check Your Work   18

Section **C**   **Let the Good Times Roll**

    Chancy Business   20
    Now We're Rolling!   21
    Tossing and Turning   22
    Think B4 You Act   23
    Find the Chance   23
    Summary   24
    Check Your Work   24

Section **D**   **Let Me Count the Ways**

    Families   26
    Robert's Clothes   27
    Hillary's Clothes   27
    Two Children Again   28
    Open or Closed?   29
    Sum It Up   29
    Treasure   31
    Summary   32
    Check Your Work   32

Additional Practice   34

Answers to Check Your Work   37

Dear Student,

You are about to begin the study of the *Mathematics in Context* unit *Take a Chance*. Think about the following words and what they mean to you: *fair, sure, uncertain, unlikely*, and *impossible*. In this unit, you will see how these words are used in mathematics.

You will toss coins and roll number cubes and record the outcomes. Do you think you can predict how many times a coin will come up heads if you toss it a certain number of times? Is the chance of getting heads greater than the chance of getting tails? As you investigate these ideas, you are beginning the study of probability.

When several different things can happen, you will learn how to count all of the possibilities in a smart way. During the next few weeks, keep alert for statements about chance you may read or hear, such as "The chance of rain is 50%." You might even keep a record of such statements and bring them to share with the class.

We hope you enjoy learning about chance!

Sincerely,

The Mathematics in Context Development Team

Section Focus

Students evaluate the fairness of decisions made in a number of real-life contexts. They explore theoretical and experimental chance, using number cubes, spinners, coins, and other objects. The instructional focus of Section A is to:

- review and apply the terms *fair* and *chance*;
- conduct simple probability experiments; and
- explore a variety of tools for making a fair decision.

Pacing and Planning

Day 1: Hillary and Robert		Student pages 1–3
INTRODUCTION	Problem 1	Discuss the definition of *chance*.
CLASSWORK	Problems 2–9	Explore and discuss the concept of *fair* in different contexts.
HOMEWORK	Problems 10–12	Describe a number cube and its uses for making fair decisions.

Day 2: Making a Spinner		Student pages 4, 5, 8
ACTIVITY	Problems 13–17	Experiment with spinners to explore fairness in making decisions.
HOMEWORK	Check Your Work Problems 1 and 2	Student Self-Assessment: Fair situations

Day 3: Different Chance Objects		Student pages 6–9
ACTIVITY	Problem 18	Experiment with irregularly shaped objects to determine if they can be used to make a fair decision.
CLASSWORK	Problems 19–21	Discuss fairness in realistic situations.
HOMEWORK	Check Your Work Problems 3 and 4	Student Self-Assessment: Evaluating and designing fair methods and tools

Additional Resources: Additional Practice, Section A, page 34

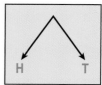

Materials

Student Resources
Quantities listed are per student.

- Letter to the Family

Teachers' Resources
Quantities listed are per class.

- Bottle cap
- Board eraser
- Copy of spinner
  (Student Book page 6)

- Large paper cup
- Small paper cup

Student Materials
Quantities listed are per pair of students, unless otherwise noted.

- Brad
- Coin
- Compass
- Drawing paper
  (three sheets per student)
- Number cube

- Paper clip
- Protractor
- Ruler
- Six-sided pencil
- Spinner
- Tacks, two

*See Hints and Comments for optional materials.

Learning Lines

Concepts *Chance* and *Fair*

This section is on fairness; the concept of chance is always related to fair in this section.

The term *chance* is used explicitly only a few times in this section.

In the beginning of the unit, students are asked to describe what they think the word *chance* means.

Later, for instance when students describe what is meant by *fair* or when students describe how they can determine whether a particular method for making decisions will be fair, students may spontaneously use the word *chance*.

The word *chance* is explicitly used in the context of tossing coins. Here an "informally" numerical value is connected to chance. It is stated that "there's a 50-50 chance of getting heads or tails." In Section A except for this example, no numerical values are connected to chance.

In the summary the word *chance* is used in the definition of fair.

Making Fair Decisions

Students explore if and how coins, number cubes, spinners, and irregular objects like paper cups can be used to make fair decisions.

They informally deal with theoretical chance when reasoning about the fairness of different methods to make decisions, like rolling number cubes, tossing coins, and spinning spinners.

This is a typical example of such a problem:

> Hillary and Robert have a black-and-white cube. Hillary wins if it comes up white, and Robert wins if it comes up black. How can you tell if the cube has been colored in a fair way?

For this type of problem students do not need to do experiments; they can find the answers by reasoning about chances.

Doing experiments with "chance objects" and recording the results is a preparation for dealing with experimental chance. The experiments are done in this section, but chance is connected to the outcomes later in Section C. At that point students have seen ways to calculate chance and express it as a number.

Models

The tree diagram is introduced in this section. It is introduced as a visual model to show all possible outcomes. In the rest of the unit, this model will be used to count all possible and favorable outcomes.

At the End of This Section: Learning Outcomes

Students are able to decide how to make fair decisions in given situations in different ways. Students can judge whether methods to make decisions are fair.

Fair

Problem 1 is the first example of a reflection item. These items appear in each section and give every student an opportunity to reflect on prior knowledge or to apply new knowledge. Teachers need to closely examine student responses to each reflection item; it provides an informal opportunity to assess student understanding and to inform instruction.

1 Make a chart of student responses that you can post and refer back to throughout the unit.

It's acceptable if students don't use fractions or percents here. These topics will be discussed later.

Fair

Hillary and Robert

This unit follows Hillary and Robert, students at Eagle Middle School in Maine, as they experiment with using chance to make decisions.

Hillary   Robert

You probably already know some things about **chance**.

1. Reflect What do you think of when someone says the word *chance*?

Reaching All Learners

Vocabulary Building

Begin a vocabulary section in Student Notebooks with the word *chance*. Add more words as you progress through this unit.

English Language Learners

In student notebooks have English Language Learners put a picture next to the word that helps students relate the meaning of the word to that picture.

Solutions and Samples

1. Answers will vary. Sample student responses:

    - I think of the chances of rain. For example, there is a 40% chance that it will rain tomorrow.

    - I think of the chances of our team winning the next game. For example, there is a 50-50 chance that our team will win the next game.

    - I think of the chances of winning the lottery. For example, the chances of winning the lottery are very small.

Hints and Comments

Overview

Students describe what the word *chance* means to them.

About the Mathematics

Problem 1 will help you evaluate students' knowledge of probability. Students will have some intuitive understanding of chance concepts as expressed in everyday language such as, "it will probably happen" or "it probably won't happen."

Planning

You may have a short class discussion about problem 1 to introduce this first section.

Comments About the Solutions

1. Students' personal experiences will vary. Some students may describe chance in general terms (a small chance, a sure thing), while others may use more exact language (a 10% chance). A 100% chance means that there is a certainty that something will happen.

Notes

2 and 3 Have a class discussion where students share situations when fairness is important.

2 and 3 Some students may suggest methods that are unfair. You may want to record on the board the methods students propose and discuss whether or not each method is fair.

8 Make a chart listing when it is important to be fair. This can be posted and referred to during the unit. Continue to add to charts as you work through this section.

Choosing

During lunch, Hillary and Robert both want to play Super Math Whiz III, a computer game. The game is installed on one computer in the classroom. Since only one person can play at a time, Hillary and Robert have to decide who will play the game first.

2. How could you solve this problem in a **fair** way?

3. What do you think it means for something to be fair?

There are many situations in which you have to find a fair way to make a decision.

Robert says to Hillary, "If you throw a 6 with this number cube, you can play; otherwise, I'll play."

4. Do you think this is fair? Why or why not?

5. Can you come up with a better way to decide?

Hillary and Robert finally decide to use a spinner like the one shown here. They decide to spin once. If the arrow points to purple, Hillary will go first. If the arrow points to green, Robert will go first.

6. Is this a fair method? Why or why not?

By now, everyone in Hillary and Robert's class has heard about the computer game and wants to play. Hillary says, "Okay, okay! Let's put all of our names in a hat, and the person whose name is drawn gets to play."

7. Is this fair? Why or why not?

A method for choosing is *fair* if it gives everyone the same chance of being chosen.

8. Think of two other situations in which it is important to be fair.

Reaching All Learners

Vocabulary Building

There are many definitions of *fair*. Make sure that the students understand the mathematical definition has nothing to do with opinion.

Hands-On Learning

Have students choose a number from 1 to 6 and then roll the number cube several times and record the results. Does this appear to be "fair" if any number is chosen?

Create a spinner like the one shown; have students actually spin it and then discuss if the spins lead to a fair result.

Solutions and Samples

2. Answers will vary. Sample student responses:
   - by flipping a coin,
   - by rolling a number cube (each person gets three numbers),
   - by spinning a spinner (with the sections of the spinner equally divided between the two players).

3. Answers will vary. Sample student responses:
   - Fair means that everyone has an equal chance of being chosen or of winning.
   - Fair means that each number on a number cube has an equal chance of coming up.
   - Fair means that when a student is chosen to run an errand, the teacher does not play favorites.
   - Fair means taking turns so that no one is left out.

4. This is not fair. A 6 will come up much less often than the other five numbers.

5. Answers will vary. Sample student responses:
   - Divide the six numbers on the number cube equally between Hillary and Robert. For example, assign the numbers 1, 2, and 3 to Hillary and the numbers 4, 5, and 6 to Robert.
   - Toss a coin. If it lands on heads, Hillary goes first, and if it lands on tails, Robert goes first.
   - Divide sections of a spinner equally between the two players. Then spin the spinner to see who will play first.

6. The method is fair. Explanations will vary. Sample explanation:

   The chance of spinning purple is equal to the chance of spinning green because the spinner is divided into two equal sections.

7. Answers will vary. Sample response:

   This is a fair method only if all the names are written on pieces of paper that are the same size and if everyone's name is put into the hat only once (or an equal number of times).

8. Answers will vary. Students' two responses may include the following:
   - when dividing food,
   - when choosing teams,
   - when judging a contest,
   - when grading students' papers.

Hints and Comments

Overview

Students solve a familiar problem: how to decide in a fair way who will play first in a game. They also discuss how to make decisions in a fair way, using a number cube or a spinner or taking names out of a hat.

About the Mathematics

Students should be allowed to explore what the word *fair* means, and what it might mean in the context of chance. Determining what is fair and what is not fair motivates the discussion of chance. This will lead to the study of the number of possible outcomes, using different objects, such as number cubes and spinners.

For a decision-making method to be fair, not only must the possible outcomes be divided equally between the two students, but each outcome must be as likely as any other. For example, look at these two spinners:

Each spinner is divided into two parts, but the spinner on the right is not fair because landing on purple is more likely than landing on green. A similar situation arises in problem 4. The method used to determine who will play the game first is unfair because the outcomes are not divided equally between the two players.

Comments About the Solutions

4. Although some students may use phrases such as *one out of six*, do not use fractions at this point. Fractions will be introduced in Section B.

Notes

Fair Again

Hillary and Robert both want to play the computer game again the next day. They decide to toss a coin to see who will play first. Since there is an equal chance (sometimes called a 50-50 chance) of getting either heads or tails, this is a fair method.

You can draw a diagram with branches like a tree to show the two possibilities. The path you take on the **tree diagram** depends on the side of the coin that comes up.

9b Have students share examples of times that there is a 50–50 chance of reaching a particular outcome.

9. **a.** What do the **H** and the **T** stand for?

   b. Robert says, "You know, the diagram shows there's a 50-50 chance of getting heads or tails." Explain what Robert means.

Look at a number cube.

10b Have students show examples of each of their strategies.

10. **a.** How many different numbers can you roll on a number cube?

    b. Draw a diagram to show the different possibilities.

11. How could Robert and Hillary use a number cube to decide in a fair way who will play the game first?

12. Hillary and Robert have a black-and-white cube. Hillary wins if it comes up white, and Robert wins if it comes up black. How can you tell if the cube has been colored in a fair way?

Reaching All Learners

Intervention

Students who have not had experience with benchmark percents may have difficulty with problem 9b and the concept of a 50-50 chance. It may help if you tell them that when a coin is tossed 100 times, you expect the coin to land on heads about 50 times and to land on tails about 50 times. This problem requires an informal understanding of percent.

Advanced Learners

For students who quickly grasp the ideas of 50-50 chance, have them work on problem 12 and ask them to figure the chances based on all different combinations of black and white faces of the cube. For example, if one face is black and five are white, there is a 1–6 chance of rolling black.

Solutions and Samples

9. a. H stands for heads; T for tails.

  b. 50–50 means that heads and tails have equal chances of coming up when a coin is tossed.

10. a. Six.

  b. Diagrams will vary. Sample student drawings:

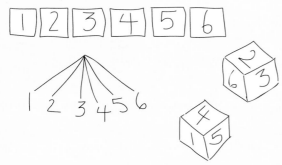

11. Answers will vary. Sample response:

Three numbers may be assigned to each person. For example, Hillary could get 1, 2, and 3, while Robert gets 4, 5, and 6. They roll the number cube. The person whose number comes up goes first.

12. There must be three white and three black sides. There are many possibilities. The sides with the numbers 1, 2, and 3 could be colored black. The sides with the numbers 4, 5, and 6 could be colored white.

Hints and Comments

Materials

number cubes (one per group of students); drawing paper (two sheets per group of students); scissors, optional (one pair per group of students); paste or glue, optional (one bottle per group)

Overview

Students explore tossing a coin or rolling a number cube or a black and white cube to determine how they could fairly decide who should play a computer game first. They also draw diagrams to show the possible outcomes of tossing a coin and rolling a number cube.

About the Mathematics

A simple tree diagram is used to show the two possible outcomes of tossing a coin. It is not necessary to discuss this model extensively at this time. Students investigate tree diagrams in greater depth in Section D.

Planning

After students finish problem 12, they should have a good understanding of the concept of fair and be able to explain what is fair in different real-life situations. If students are having difficulty with the concept, discuss problems 4, 5, 10, and 11 with the whole class.

Comments About the Solutions

  9. b. Students' answers will show their informal knowledge about percents and chance. Fifty-fifty refers to the percent chance of a coin's landing on heads or on tails.

  10. The problem covers the same topic as problem 9—picturing all possible outcomes—but now there are six possible outcomes instead of two.

Notes

Hillary's class is studying dinosaurs. The teacher, Mr. Lotto, would like the students to report on dinosaur bones found in different parts of the world.

Mr. Lotto decides to divide the world into three regions (see the map on page 5):

* North America, South America, and Antarctica;

* Europe and Africa; and

* Asia and Australia.

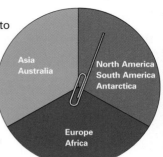

The students in the class think it will be fair if they use a spinner to assign one of these regions to each of them.

Activity

Making a Spinner

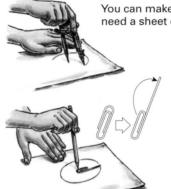

You can make your own spinner that looks like this one. You will need a sheet of paper, a paper clip, and a compass.

* Draw a circle on a blank sheet of paper with the compass. Mark the point in the middle.

* Take a paper clip and straighten one end.

* Use a pencil to hold the paper clip over the center of the circle.

* Divide the spinner into three equal parts as shown. Write the name of one of the regions in each part.

Spin the spinner 15 times. Record the results.

13. Some students may recognize the pie pieces in the picture of the spinner and use fractions to represent chance. Using fractions to represent chance is discussed in Section B.

Suggest that students make a tally sheet or chart to record their results.

13. Can you tell from your results whether your spinner can be used to make fair decisions? Explain.

Reaching All Learners

Intervention

Struggling students would benefit from pre-made tables like the ones shown in the Solutions and Samples section of this page.

Solutions and Samples

13. Results and answers will vary. Sample responses:

Outcome	Number of Times It Came Up
North and South America, and Antarctica	|||
Asia and Australia	卌 ||
Europe and Africa	卌

You cannot tell from the results that the spinner is fair. But the spinner is divided into three equal parts, and each part has an equal chance of coming up. So the spinner is fair.

Hints and Comments

Materials

brads, compasses, drawing paper, paper clips, protractors, and rulers (one of each per group of students)

Overview

Students construct spinners and experiment with them to determine whether or not they could be used to fairly assign report topics in class.

About the Mathematics

In this activity, students are informally introduced to the concepts of angles and turns. They must realize that in order for the spinner to have equal sections, each angle must measure 120°. These concepts are studied more extensively in the geometry unit *Figuring All the Angles*.

Planning

Students may want to use a brad, rather than a pencil, to hold the paper clip in place on the spinner. Discuss the results of the spinning activity with the whole class. Encourage students to pay close attention to the outcomes and distribution of spins.

Notes

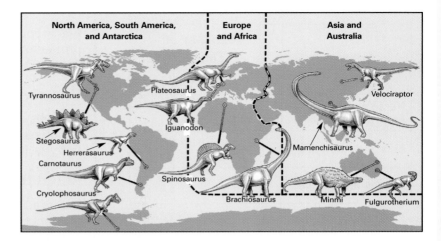

Shanna wonders whether a spinner made out of a triangle can be used to make fair decisions.

14. **a.** Draw a triangle on a sheet of paper. Can you make the triangle into a fair spinner?

b. How can you tell whether it is fair?

c. Can any triangle be made into a fair spinner? Support your answer with some examples.

Jonathan wonders if he can use a number cube to choose regions in a fair way.

15. **a.** Can he? If so, how?

b. Kara wonders if she can use a coin. Can she?

16. How can you tell whether a particular method will be fair? Explain your answer.

Since many bones were recently found in Europe and Africa, Mr. Lotto thinks more students should be reporting on this region than on each of the other regions.

17. **a.** How could you make a spinner so the region Europe and Africa is picked more often than each of the others?

b. Would this spinner be fair?

14a Students without experience with angle measurement can still draw a triangle with equal sections.

14b Discuss students' spinners in class.

16 Discuss this problem in class to promote students' explanations of fairness.

Encourage students who give a response of "test it" to be more specific.

Assessment Pyramid

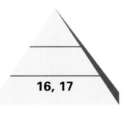

16, 17

Understand the meaning of fair and how it relates to chance.

Reaching All Learners

Intervention

For students struggling with problem 14b, you may need to put a spinner on an unfair triangle and move it slowly to help them see that it takes them longer to move through some sections than others.

Advanced Learners

Challenge students who quickly grasp the concept introduced in problem 14 to try using a spinner with a variety of geometric shapes and list the shapes that are fair and those that are unfair. Ask how they know they are fair or unfair.

Solutions and Samples

14. a. Yes. Sample student drawing:

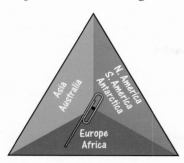

b. It is a fair spinner if the interior angles for the regions are equal. Note that the areas do not have to be equal, only the angles do. Some students may understand this point. Sample student drawing:

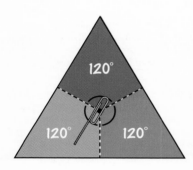

c. Yes. The only requirement is that the spinner be divided into equal angles. Allow students to experiment.

15. a. A number cube will work if each region is assigned two numbers on the cube.

b. A coin has only two outcomes, so it will not work.

16. A fair method has a total number of outcomes that is divisible by three, with each outcome having the same chance of occurring.

17. a. You could make the central angle that represents Europe and Africa larger than the central angles for the other regions. Another possibility is to divide the spinner into more than three equal sections and give Europe and Africa more sections than the other regions.

b. No, this spinner would not be fair for all regions.

Hints and Comments

Materials

brads, compasses, drawing paper (one sheet per group of students), paper clips, protractors, and rulers (one of each per group of students)

Overview

Students construct a spinner in the shape of a triangle and determine whether or not it could be used to fairly assign class report topics. Then students consider using a number cube or a coin to assign report topics.

Comments About the Solutions

14. Note that the areas of the triangle sections do not have to be equal, but the angles around the central point do. To emphasize this point, look at a similar situation. Ask students these questions: *Have you ever seen a watch in a shape other than a circle? How could you design that watch face so it could be used to tell time?* Here are two possible answers:

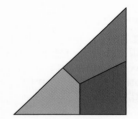

15. b. Students may try to come up with elaborate schemes for using a coin, but theses schemes will probably not offer equal chances.

17. As in problem 14, the sizes of the central angles, not the areas of the sections, are important.

Notes

Hillary wonders what other objects can be used to make fair decisions. When objects are not shaped as regularly as coins, number cubes, or spinners, it can be hard to tell. One way to find out is to flip or spin the object over and over again to see what happens each time.

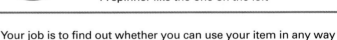

Activity

Different Chance Objects

Your teacher will divide the class into groups. Each group will get one of the items listed below:

- A large paper cup
- A small paper cup
- A chalkboard eraser
- A bottle cap
- A spinner like the one on the left

Your job is to find out whether you can use your item in any way to make a fair decision.

18. Toss or spin your item 30 times. Make a table of your results. When you are done, decide whether you can use your item to make a fair decision. Report your results to the class. Keep these results because you will use them again later in the unit.

18 Set ground rules for coin tossing; for example, it must land on a desk and don't toss the coin too high.

You may want to discuss the possible outcomes of each object with the group using it.

Be sure the results are kept in a safe place to use with problem 14 in Section C.

The Concert

Compass Rose, a rock band Hillary likes, is coming to play in Eagle next week. Hillary's mother got four tickets to the concert. She will take Hillary and two of Hillary's friends.

Unfortunately, Hillary has three friends she wants to bring, and she has to find a fair way to decide who will go with her.

Reaching All Learners

Accommodation

The easiest item to toss or spin is a spinner; the most difficult is the paper cup. Assign items to students that will be the most appropriate for them to use.

Have a variety of circles available for students to use as spinners if they are having difficulty drawing their own.

Intervention

Students may wish to share their tables on the board or overhead so that others may copy them if they are having difficulty drawing their own.

Solutions and Samples

18. The cups and eraser cannot be used to make a fair decision, while the spinner can be used in such a way. The bottle cap may or may not be used to make a fair decision, depending on the individual bottle cap.

Sample student tables:

Cup: 3 trials

Side	26	27	28
Top	3	3	1
Bottom	1	0	1

Eraser: 4 trials

Side 1	5	3	1	2
Side 2	4	0	6	2
Top	10	15	9	14
Bottom	11	12	14	12

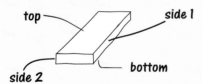

The eraser never got on the short sides.

Hints and Comments

Materials

a bottle cap, a chalkboard eraser, large and small paper cups, and one copy of the spinner on Student Book page 6

Overview

Students experiment with irregularly shaped objects and determine whether or not these objects can be used to make fair decisions.

About the Mathematics

Regularly shaped objects offer equal chances of landing on any given side; these chances can be calculated in advance. The objects students use in this activity have irregular shapes; therefore, the chances of the possible outcomes must be determined experimentally.

The notion of theoretical versus experimental chances is introduced in the unit *Second Chance*. This activity may be used to introduce the idea that variability occurs in any probability situation. If more than one group uses the same item, discuss the similarities and differences in the results. For example, when flipping a bottle cap 50 times, two groups got these results:

	H	T
Group 1	26	24
Group 2	23	27

You may ask students if this is what they would have expected and to explain why or why not.

Planning

Prepare the materials for this activity in advance. You can have each group experiment with more than one item. Ask students to save their work because this activity will be used again in Section C.

Comments About the Solutions

18. The number of outcomes for each object depends on whether or not you accept some of the more unlikely flips as possibilities. If all outcomes are acceptable, then the cap and spinner have two outcomes each, the cup has three outcomes, and the eraser has six outcomes (although the possibility of the eraser landing on an end is very unlikely).

Notes

21b Ask struggling students what would happen if there were 2 boys and 15 girls in the class. This may help make the problem easier for them to understand.

21c and 21d Take this opportunity to discuss the difference between mathematical fairness (problem c) and opinion (problem d).

19. Find a fair way to decide which two friends will go with Hillary. You may use coins, number cubes, spinners, or anything else you think may be fair.

Oh no! Another of Hillary's friends wants to go too!

20. Come up with a fair way to decide which two of the four will go with Hillary now.

21. Give your opinion about the fairness of each of the following situations:

   a. A referee tosses a coin before a game to see which of two soccer teams gets to choose a goal.

   b. In Mr. Ryan's class, there are 10 boys and 15 girls. To decide who will be hall monitors each day, Mr. Ryan draws the name of one girl from a box holding all of the girls' names and then draws the name of one boy from a box holding all of the boys' names.

   c. Only 50 students can go on a field trip to the zoo because there is only one bus. The principal decides to allow the first 50 who sign up before school in the morning to go on the trip.

   d. In the United States, all people 18 years old or older are eligible to vote for a presidential candidate.

Assessment Pyramid

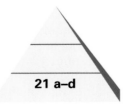

21 a–d

Understand the meaning of fair and how it relates to chance.

Reaching All Learners

Act It Out

Divide the class into four groups and have each group act out the four scenarios presented in problem 21. Discuss as a whole class.

Advanced Learners

Students who have a good grasp of the scenarios in problem 21 may want to write a paragraph explaining the fairness of each one; then match the paragraph with the actual results to see if in fact they are the same.

Solutions and Samples

19. Answers will vary. Sample responses:

- Using a number cube, assign two different numbers to each friend. Roll the number cube 30 times and record the results. The two friends whose numbers come up most often get to go with Hillary.
- Divide a spinner into three equal sections. Spin the spinner to choose friends. On the second spin, if the spinner lands on the name of the friend already chosen, spin the spinner again until a second friend is chosen.
- Write the friends' names on pieces of paper of equal size. Put their names in a hat and choose one.

20. Answers will vary. The easiest method is to write the four friends' names on pieces of paper and draw their names from a hat. A spinner divided into four equal sections could also be used.

21. a. This is a fair situation. Sample explanations:

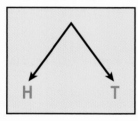

- There is an equal chance of getting either heads or tails on the coin toss.
- There is a 50-50 chance of heads or tails coming up.
- The diagram shows that their chances are equal.

b. This is not a fair situation. In this method, boys have a higher chance of being chosen because there are fewer boys in the class.

c. This is not fair because some students may not be able to get to school early. Everyone does not have an equal chance.

d. Answers will vary. This is not a question of mathematical fairness, but one of opinion. Again, this problem may require discussion about whether or not people under 18 should be allowed to vote.

21. d. Any person 18 years or older can vote for any presidential candidate. So, the elections are mathematically fair. Of course, many other factors play a role.

Hints and Comments

Materials

coins, number cubes or or spinners (one of each per group of students)

Overview

Students decide which method they will use to choose who will go to a rock concert when a limited number of tickets is available. Students also give their opinions about the fairness of real-life situations.

About the Mathematics

In these problems, students focus on the number of possible outcomes. The method for choosing must have the same number (or a multiple of it) of possible outcomes as the number of choices. If all outcomes are equally likely in a situation, it is fair.

Planning

After students complete problem 19, they should be able to explain how to use spinners, coins, or number cubes to make fair decisions.

Comments About the Solutions

19. A spinner with three equal sections can be used. If the first person's name reoccurs, repeated trials may have to be conducted to select the second person. A more direct approach using the spinner is to choose the person who will not go.

A coin is difficult to use in this problem. Some students may try to solve the problem by tossing a coin, assigning heads for friend A and tails for friends B and C. If tails comes up on the first toss, friends B and C get to go with Hillary. If heads comes up on the first toss, friend A gets to go and a second toss is required to decide between friends B and C. With this method, friend A has a 50% chance of being picked, while friends B and C have only a 25% chance each.

20. It is possible to solve this problem by tossing two coins. It is not very likely that students will come up with this method, because some students may fail to realize that there are four possible outcomes: HH, HT, TH, and TT. Many students might say there are three possible outcomes: TT, HH, and either HT or TH.

21. a. Part a presents the same situation as problem 9.

b. In part b, Mr. Ryan probably wants to pick one boy and one girl. Because there are fewer boys than girls, a boy has a greater chance of being chosen. Some students may respond that a boy has a 1 out of 10 chance of being chosen, and a girl has a 1 out of 15 chance of being chosen.

Notes

The summary on this page is critical because it introduces an informal definition of *fair*.

After having a student read the summary aloud, you may wish to have them go back through the section and find problems that support the concepts taught. This will encourage students to actively use the summary section as a study tool.

Be sure to discuss Check Your Work with the students so they understand when to give themselves credit for an answer that is different from the one at the back of the book.

1 You can either have students reason about this or try it out themselves. If you do not want students to use tacks, demonstrate flipping a tack on an overhead projector. The shadow of the tack can easily be seen.

 Fair

Summary

There are many situations in daily life that involve **chance** or require you to make **fair** decisions. *Fair* means that every possibility has the same chance of occurring.

In order to make fair decisions, you should use a fair method. Things that can help you make fair decisions are coins, number cubes, and spinners. Many other objects can also help you make fair decisions.

Check Your Work

1. **a.** Can you toss a pencil to make a fair decision? Explain your answer.

   b. Can you toss a thumbtack to make a fair decision? Explain your answer.

Hillary is riding her bike. She is on her way to visit one of her friends. She has not yet decided if she will visit Laura or Asja. Hillary decides, "If the next traffic light is green, I will visit Asja; otherwise, I will visit Laura."

2. Is this a fair way to decide? Explain.

Three students from Hillary's class want to play a game. They need to decide who will go first in the game.

3. Describe how they can make a fair decision in each of the following ways:

   a. using a number cube

   b. using a spinner (Also draw a spinner they can use.)

   c. using one coin (This is not easy!)

   d. using another way (Decide on this way yourself.)

Every week, a quiz show on television features two competing teams from local schools. A participating school may send 40 students to sit in the audience. The principal of Eagle Middle School has decided that each of the eight classes in the school should hold a drawing to select five students who will go to the studio.

Assessment Pyramid

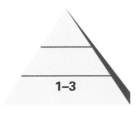

1–3

Assesses Section A Goals

Reaching All Learners

Parent Involvement

Have students discuss the Summary and Check Your Work with their parents. Parents often wish to help their child and may benefit from helping to look for problems from the section that support the Check Your Work problems.

Solutions and Samples

Answers to Check Your Work

1. **a.** Yes, a pencil can be used for fair decisions if:

    1) the pencil has regularly shaped sides,

    2) the chance of landing on the eraser is very small,

    3) you number the sides.

    You might find out by flipping a pencil 100 times, or just by looking at its sides.

   b. No. A thumbtack is too irregularly shaped to be predictable. You will have to toss it many times to determine whether or not it can be used to make a fair decision.

2. This is hard to determine. It is fair only if the traffic light is green for the same amount of time that it is not green. This does not seem very likely.

3. **a.** A number cube can be used to decide who goes first if each student is assigned two numbers. For instance, student A is assigned 1 and 2; student B, 3 and 4; and student C, 5 and 6. A number cube can also be used if each student is assigned only one number. If an unassigned number comes up, the cube is rolled again. For instance, student A is assigned 1; student B, 2; and student C, 3. If a 4, 5, or 6 shows, the cube is rolled again until a 1, 2, or 3 shows.

   b. A spinner can be used if it is divided into three equal parts and each student is assigned one of the parts.

   c. This is a hard problem: It is possible to use one coin, but you will have to design a clever way to make decisions. For instance, the following method can be used:

   Round 1: Toss the coin three times, once for each student. If it comes up heads, the student has lost and will not go first. If it comes up tails, the student is still in the running. If all three tosses come up heads, start over. If more than one student is still in, go to round 2.

   Round 2: Repeat round 1. Toss the coin once for each remaining student. Continue until only one student remains. He or she will go first in the game.

   d. Different answers are possible. One might be to write each student's name on a piece of paper, put the names in a hat or a box, and draw one name.

Hints and Comments

Materials

six-sided pencils (one per group of students), tacks (two per group of students)

Overview

Students read the Summary, which reviews the main concepts covered in this section. In Check Your Work they assess themselves on the concepts and skills from this section. Students can check their answers on pages 37–38 of the *Take a Chance* Student Book.

Planning

After students complete Section A, you may assign for homework appropriate activities from the Additional Practice section, located on pages 34–36 of the *Take a Chance* Student Book.

Comments About the Solutions

2. Besides the number of possible outcomes—green, yellow, red on the traffic light—the time each color is shown is important to decide if Hillary's method is fair.

3. This problem is connected to a number of problems in the section. It revisits the ways different objects can be used in different ways to make fair decisions.

 **Fair**

Notes

4 This problem is similar to problem 21b.

For Further Reflection
Reflective questions are meant to summarize and discuss important concepts.

Here is a list of the eight classes at Eagle School.

Class	Number of Students	Number Selected
Mr. Johnson	75	5
Mr. Geist	77	5
Ms. Lanie	50	5
Ms. McCall	51	5
Mr. Ford	74	5
Ms. Durden	75	5
Mr. Shore	70	5
Mr. Luxe	52	5

The principal says her method is fair.

4. **a.** Is the principal's method fair?

b. If you were a student at Eagle Middle School, in which class would you want to be?

c. Hillary and Robert have decided to design a different method that will be fair for the principal to use. What method do you think they might design?

 For Further Reflection

You have been asked to choose a method for making a fair decision. Think of a situation that would require a fair decision and describe at least three methods you could use.

Assessment Pyramid

4, ☐FFR

Assesses Section A Goals

Reaching All Learners

Extension

Have students play the following game. Then challenge them to find out why the game is unfair. The game is played with two players. Player 1 starts by saying the number "one." Player 2 must increase the number by one or two. Player 1 then increases the number by one or two. The two players take turns. The winner is the first person to say "ten." (The game is unfair because Player 1 can always win by saying the numbers one, four, seven, and ten.)

Solutions and Samples

4. a. No, because students in different classes do not have the same chance of being chosen.

b. Ms. Lanie's class. A student in the class with the fewest total students has the best chance of being chosen.

c. Answers will vary. One fair method would be to put the names of all of the students in the school in one hat, mix up the names, and pick 40 names from the hat without looking.

For Further Reflection

Some examples of situations that require a fair decision:

- decide who will start a game,
- decide who gets tickets for a concert,
- decide who may represent the class in a contest.

Spinners, coins, and number cubes are some examples of methods that can be used.

Hints and Comments

4. This problem is similar to 21b. Some students may use fractions to compare the chance of being picked. This is an opportunity to discuss how fractions with the same numerator but different denominators can be compared. If two fractions have the same numerator, the fraction with the smaller denominator represents the class in which a student has a better chance of being selected.

For Further Reflection

Students may want to explore how the number of outcomes influences the method selected. For example, if a decision between two people or teams needs to be made, flipping a coin is appropriate. However, if five friends are trying to decide who gets tickets for a concert, picking names out of a hat might be the preferred method.

The instructional focus of Section B is to:

- **use visual models to estimate and calculate chance and**
- **calculate and express chance for simple situations using percents, fractions, or ratios.**

Pacing and Planning

Day 4: Up and Down Events		Student pages 10–12
INTRODUCTION	Problem 1	Estimate the chance that an event will occur.
CLASSWORK	Problems 2–4	Estimate chance by placing events on a chance ladder.
HOMEWORK	Problem 5	Calculate chance for events and place events on a chance ladder.

Day 5: Frog Newton		Student pages 13–15
INTRODUCTION	Problem 6 and 7	Estimate the chance of a jumping frog landing on a particular square.
CLASSWORK	Problems 8–11	Use an area model to calculate chance and record the results on a chance ladder.
HOMEWORK	Problems 12 and 13	Use an area model to represent and calculate chance.

Day 6: Spinners		Student pages 16–19
INTRODUCTION	Problems 14–16	Identify spinners that can be used to make fair decisions.
CLASSWORK	Problem 17	Find newspaper headlines that include statements of chance and place the headlines on a chance ladder.
HOMEWORK	Check Your Work, Problems 1–4	Student Self-Assessment

Day 7: Assessment		Student pages 16–19
REVIEW	Sections A and B	Review Summary pages from Section A and B.
ASSESSMENT	Quiz 1	Assesses Section A and B Goals.

Additional Resources: Additional Practice, Section B, Student pages 34 and 35

Materials

Student Resources

Quantities listed are per student.

- Student Activity Sheets 1–3

Teachers' Resources

No resources required.

Student Materials

Quantities listed are per pair of students, unless otherwise noted.

- Black crayon (one per student)
- Drawing paper (four sheets per student)
- Newspaper

* See Hints and Comments for optional materials.

Learning Lines

Chance as Having a Numerical Value

In this section, students gain a basic understanding of the concept of chance by estimating chances and describing them using qualitative descriptions such as "sure" and "not sure," before describing exact chances using percents, fractions, or ratios.

Students estimate and express chance first in terms like "sure to happen," "sure not to happen," and "not sure." They order chances along this dimension using a visual model, the chance ladder.

When ordering chances within the category "not sure," students need to find a way to compare the chances and thus refine this category. This will help develop the understanding that chances can be expressed with a number.

When students order chances that can be calculated, this will give them an idea on how to find the numerical value of a chance. Students do not need to *master* "calculating chances" at this stage. This will be dealt with repeatedly later in this unit as well as in the following unit in this strand: *A Second Chance.*

Ways to Express Chance

In this section, chance is first expressed in everyday qualitative language like: "It is sure to happen;" "It probably will;" "There's a 50-50 chance." Next, chance is expressed quantitatively as a percentage, by placing chances on a ladder with a scale ranging from 0% to 100%. This is done only for simple percentages, like 50% and 25%, and by ordering.

Chance is also expressed as a ratio "so many out of so many." This ratio is connected to the corresponding fraction. A connection is made to Section A by having students order chances for spinners. Here students cannot use the ratio notation based on counting. They can, however, use fractions and thus connect ratio and fractions. Students need to have some basic ability in working with benchmark fractions, percents, and ratios and relate these to one another.

Models

The chance ladder is introduced as a visual model to express and order chances on a scale from "sure not to happen" to "sure to happen," with nine rungs in between.

On the same ladder, later a scale ranging from 0% to 100% is added to the qualitative scale. Then each rung can be assigned a value as a percentage in multiples of 10%.

The ladder is then modeled into a scale line ranging from 0%–100%.

Students are also asked to put fractions on the scale.

The model is slowly evolving from a model of a situation to a model for ordering chances. The scale line on the right, which uses only the percents, is like a number line.

At the End of This Section

Students are able to order chances and express chance using ratios, fractions, or percents.

1 Read and discuss each statement with the class. Some answers may reflect unusual situations. Give students an opportunity to justify their answers.

1e Remind students that a year has 365 days and a leap year has 366 days. So, there are 366 different days for a birthday.

B

What's the Chance?

Up and Down Events

Sometimes it is difficult to predict whether an event will take place. Other times you know for sure.

1. Use **Student Activity Sheet 1**. Put a check in the column that best describes your confidence that each event will take place.

	Statement	Sure It Won't	Not Sure	Sure It Will
A	You will have a test in math sometime this year.			
B	It will rain in your town sometime in the next four days.			
C	The number of students in your class who can roll their tongues will equal the number of students who cannot.			
D	You will roll a 7 with a normal number cube.			
E	In a room of 367 people, two people will have the same birthday.			
F	New Year's Day will come on the third Monday in January.			
G	When you toss a coin once, heads will come up.			
H	If you enter "2 + 2 =" on your calculator, the result will be 4.			

Reaching All Learners

Extension

Students may enjoy writing some of their own statements. Have them share their ideas in small groups and have the group members decide if they think the statement will or won't happen.

English Language Learners

You will find it helpful to read these aloud, one at a time for students who have difficulty reading. Clarify each statement before moving on to the next statement.

Solutions and Samples

1. Answers will vary for some statements. Sample student responses:

   a. Sure it will.

   b. Not sure. (This may depend on the time of year or where students live.)

   c. Not sure.

   d. Sure it won't.

   e. Sure it will. (For 366 people, the answer would be "not sure" because each person could have his or her birthday on a different day, including February 29 during leap years. For 367 people, two birthdays must fall on the same day.)

   f. Sure it won't.

   g. Not sure.

   h. Sure it will.

Hints and Comments

Materials

Student Activity Sheet 1 (one per student)

Overview

Students think about how likely it is that eight given events will occur.

About the Mathematics

Students gain a basic understanding of the concept of chance by estimating chances and describing them using qualitative descriptions such as *sure* and *not sure*, before describing exact chances using percents, fractions, or ratios.

Students base their chance "estimates" on the general idea that some events are sure to happen, some are sure not to happen, and all the other possibilities are between these two extremes.

On the next page, students think about various intermediary positions.

Notes

Have a student read the text aloud. This text introduces the chance ladder.

2 The 10 rungs of the ladder correspond to the 10% benchmark and its multiples, with 0% at ground level and 100% at the highest rung. Do not point this out to students yet. This concept is introduced on the next page.

3 Students should now be able to order the likeliness of the events they were not sure about from problem 1.

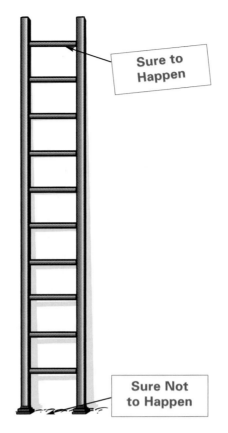

Sure to Happen

Sure Not to Happen

If you are wondering about the chance a particular event will happen, thinking about a ladder may help.

If you are pretty sure something will occur, you can think of it as being near the top of the ladder.

If you are pretty sure something will not occur, you can think of it as being near the bottom of the ladder.

If you are sure something will not happen, you can think of it as being on the ground!

You can mark on a drawing of a ladder how great the chance is a particular event will occur.

2. Draw a ladder like the one on the left. Put the three statements below on your ladder.

   a. The next car you see on the road will have been built in the United States.

   b. A gorilla will visit your school tomorrow.

   c. Your fingernails will grow today.

3. Now go back to the table on page 10 and put the statements from the table on one ladder. Explain why you put the statements where you did.

4. Put the following statements about chance on a ladder:

   "I'm sure it will happen."   "There's a 50-50 chance."

   "That's unlikely."   "It's very likely to happen."

   "It probably will."   "There's no way it will occur."

   "There's a 100% chance."   "It seems very unlikely."

   "There's a 0% chance."   "It could happen."

Assessment Pyramid

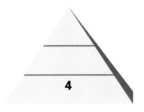

4

Estimate and order chance events.

Reaching All Learners

Intervention

Draw a chance ladder on the board or overhead. Count the rungs on the ladder. Define "Sure to Happen" and "Sure Not to Happen."

It is important that students know 0% chance and 100% chance. Have all students make a statement of their own that indicates "sure to happen" and "Sure Not to Happen."

English Language Learners

Review the terms *likely, unlikely, sure,* and *certain.* English Language Learners learners may have difficulty deciding which of these is applicable; help them by describing other situations; for example, it will be dark at night; it will not be Wednesday on the day following Monday.

Solutions and Samples

2. Ladders will vary. Sample ladder:

3. Ladders will vary. Sample student response:

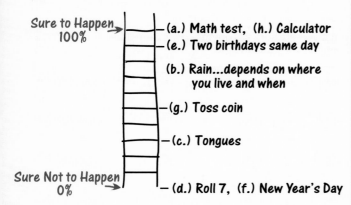

4. Ladders will vary. Sample student response:

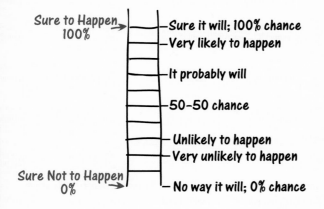

Hints and Comments

Materials

drawing paper (one sheet per group)

Overview

Students estimate the chances of different events occurring by placing each event in the appropriate place on a chance ladder.

About the Mathematics

The addition of ten rungs on the ladder makes it necessary for students to refine the category "Not Sure" of problem 1. They are still allowed to express chances in qualitative terms of being "pretty sure" that something will or will not happen in order to estimate the placement of each event on the chance ladders.

Comments About the Solutions

4. Students should be able to use the chance ladder and understand that chances occur in a range.

B What's the Chance?

Notes

You may need to review with your class the concept of percent. Elicit definitions from your students.

b Ask students for examples of numbers divisible by 5.

d Clarify the language "digits will add up to" by giving an example such as "If the number is 75, you add 7 and 5 and get 12."

5 Students should be able to use the chance ladder and understand that chances occur in a range.

Match 'Em Up

Dan is doing an experiment. He has a bag containing pieces of paper of equal size, numbered 1 to 20. He is going to pick a number from the bag. Here are some possible outcomes for the number he will pick.

    a. It will be even.

    b. It will be divisible by 5.

    c. It will be a 1 or a 2.

    d. The digits in the number will add up to 12.

    e. It will be less than 16.

5. Put the five statements on a ladder like the one on the right and explain why you put them where you did.

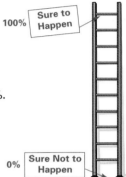

The ladder shows that the chance of an event occurring is between 0% and 100%.

* Events you are sure are going to happen will be at the top.

* Events you are sure will not happen will be at the bottom.

* Events you are not sure about will be somewhere in between.

Assessment Pyramid

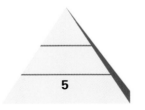

Estimate and order chance events.

Reaching All Learners

Hands-On Learning

Prepare a bag that is the same as Dan's experiment. Have students draw a number and find which of the possible scenarios fit that number.

English Language Learners

Define *divisible, digits, even.*

Intervention

Draw the divisions of the chance ladder on the board or overhead; count the number of rungs and mark each division with a number (10, 20, 30, etc.) before marking the percent sign.

Solutions and Samples

5. Ladders will vary. Sample student response:

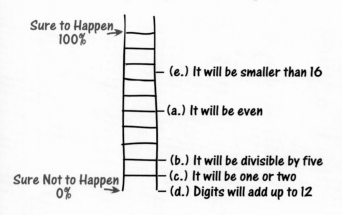

Hints and Comments

Materials

drawing paper (three sheets per group)

Overview

Students estimate the chances of events occurring by placing each event in an appropriate position on a chance ladder. The ladder shows that the chance that an event will occur is between 0% and 100%.

About the Mathematics

The use of chance ladders builds a basic understanding that chances range between 0% and 100%. Students first learn to describe chance informally by placing statements in everyday language on a chance ladder at a height that represents the chance on a 0–10 ring scale. Later each rung can be assigned a value as a percentage in multiples of 10%. Students are assumed to be familiar with simple percentages. Other ways to describe chance are by using ratio terminology (for example, *one out of six*) or fractions (1:6). Students will use this method later in the section.

Comments About the Solutions

5. The purpose of this problem is only to order the chances. Students do not need to calculate each chance exactly; allow students to make global comparisons. For example, have them compare b and c. (There are more numbers that correspond to statement b than numbers that correspond to statement c, so the chance that a number will be a 1 or a 2 is lower than the chance that it is divisible by 5.) Students have the option of calculating exact percents here, but do not make it mandatory. (You may wish to have students figure out the percents later. The actual percents are 50%, 20%, 10%, 0%, and 75%.)

Notes

Frog Newton

Hillary is walking to the science lab carrying her pet bullfrog, Newton.

Newton, in fear for his life...

...jumps out of his aquarium and hops off as fast as his little feet can carry him.

Hillary finally finds Newton. He is sitting on a tile in the hall.

6 and 7 Discuss students' responses to problems 6 and 7 with the entire class.

6. Look at the floor in the hall. Do you think Hillary found Newton sitting on a black tile or a white tile? Explain.

Hall

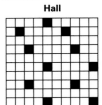

7. What if, instead, Newton was found on a tile in the cafeteria: Is it likely he was on the same color tile?

Cafeteria

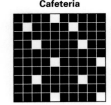

Reaching All Learners

Hands-On Learning

Students can build a floor (using tiles of any 2 colors) that exactly matches the picture. Then they can count how many there are of each color and make the ratios for the chance statements.

Advanced Learners

Make a more formal list of chance in both fraction and percent form.

Solutions and Samples

6. Newton was most likely sitting on a white tile.

7. No. There are more black tiles on the cafeteria floor, so there is a greater chance that the tile is black.

Hints and Comments

Overview

Using the context of a frog that jumps on a tile floor, students describe how likely it is that the frog will land on a black tile or a white tile, by comparing the number of black and white tiles.

About the Mathematics

The floors with black and white tiles give students visual support for estimating chances. This context prepares students to use ratio terminology for describing chances, such as *one out of four*.

Comments About the Solutions

6.–7. Some students may respond that the frog could have been sitting on either color of tiles.

Notes

8 Guide struggling students to count the total number of squares and the number of shaded squares. Relate back to their experience with writing a fraction.

8 and 9 Remind students that the frog has the ability to jump on any square no matter how far away it is.

Students do not have to compute the exact percents. They should, however, be able to estimate and compare the chances by placing each event in an appropriate position on the scale.

10a Save **SAS 2** to use again with problem 12 on page 15.

11b This problem is critical as it introduces writing chance statements as a ratio.

Here is another tile floor.

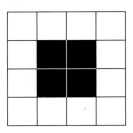

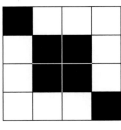

8. Suppose Newton made another dash for freedom on this floor. Draw a scale like the one here. Mark the chance Newton will end up on a black tile. Explain why you marked the scale where you did.

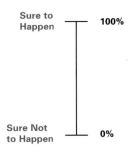

Now look at another floor.

9. **a.** On the same scale that you used for problem 8, mark the chance Newton will end up on a black tile on this floor.

   b. Is it greater or less than the chance in problem 8? Explain.

10. **a.** On **Student Activity Sheet 2**, color the first floor so Newton will have a 50% chance of landing on a black tile.

    b. Mark the 50% chance on the scale on **Student Activity Sheet 2**.

    c. What is another way of saying "The chance is 50%"?

11. **a.** For the floor in problem 8, you can say the chance Newton will end up on a black tile is 4 out of 16. Explain.

    b. Jim says, "That's the same as 1 out of 4." Do you agree? Explain.

    c. What fraction can be used to express this chance? And what percent?

    d. Here is the floor from problem 9. What is the chance Newton will end up on a black tile on this floor?

Assessment Pyramid

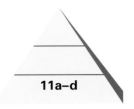

11a–d

Express chance using percents, fractions, and ratios.

Reaching All Learners

Advanced Learners

Have students color pictures of tiled floors with 3 or 4 colors on one floor and ask them to give the fraction and percent of landing on each color.

Intervention

Mark the ladder with ten rungs as in previous lessons.

Solutions and Samples

8. Answers may vary. Sample drawing:

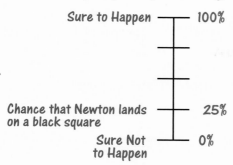

9. a. Answers may vary. Sample drawing:

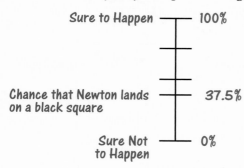

b. Bigger. In the floor for problem 8, only four out of the sixteen squares are black. In problem 9, six out of the sixteen squares are black. Since there are more black squares in problem 9 than in problem 8, it is more likely Newton will land on a black square.

10. a. Floors will vary. Accept any solution that shows one-half of the squares black and one-half of the squares white. You may want students to compare their solutions.

Sample solutions:

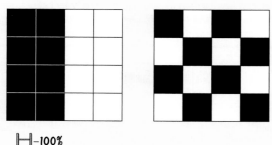

b.

c. Answers will vary. Sample responses:
- one out of two chances,
- a 50-50 chance.

Hints and Comments

Materials

black crayons (one per student),
Student Activity Sheet 2 (one per student)

Overview

Students estimate the chances that a frog will land on a black tile on different black-and-white tile floors by putting them on a percent scale. Students also interpret ratio terminology used to express these chances.

About the Mathematics

The chance ladder is now reduced to a vertical percent scale without intermediate markings. The main reference points on the scale are 0%, 50%, and 100%. Also the ratio terminology, such as *one out of four*, is introduced. To describe chance using this terminology, it is necessary that the black tiles be compared with the total number of tiles (the total number of possibilities).

Planning

Remind students to save their copy of Student Activity Sheet 2 to use again in problem 12 on page 15 of the Student Book.

Comments About the Solutions

8. Discuss students' explanations to this problem. Some students may reason that the frog has a 50% chance of landing on a black tile since the floor is made up of only black and white tiles. If no students offer this explanation, ask them to react to this statement during the discussion.

In part c students are asked to express "1 out of 4" as a fraction and a percent. Discuss this if students have difficulty. You may use a drawing like the one above.

11. d. Students are asked to find the exact chance of landing on certain tiles for the first time. All of the previous problems could be answered informally. Some students may reduce the ratio 6 out of 16 to 3 out of 8. However, this is not necessary.

11. a. Explanations may vary. Sample explanation:

There are 4 black squares and 16 total squares, so the chance of landing on a black square is 4 out of 16.

b. Yes. The ratio 1 out of 4 is the same as 4 out of 16. They are equivalent ratios.

c. $\frac{1}{4}$ or 25%

d. 6 out of 16, or 3 out of 8; $\frac{3}{8}$ or 37.5%

Notes

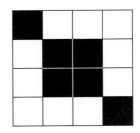

12a Ask students to share their strategies and computations before they begin coloring.

12b Ask students to show how they found the chance of landing on a black tile.

Have students share their floors with the class. If they use color, this makes a nice bulletin board display.

13 Bring the class together for a whole group discussion after this problem.

12. a. Color the second floor on **Student Activity Sheet 2** so Newton's chance of ending up on a black tile will be 1 out of 5.

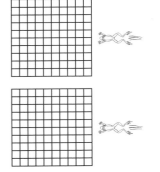

b. Now color the third floor on **Student Activity Sheet 2** with any pattern of black and white tiles. What is the chance Newton will end up on a black tile on the floor you made?

13. Reflect If you had a black-and-white tile floor, explain how you could find the chance a frog hopping around on it will stop on a black tile.

It turns out that Newton didn't have to worry. He is only part of an experiment at the science fair on the number of flies frogs eat.

Assessment Pyramid

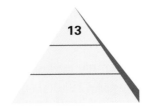

Determine theoretical probability using tile ratios.

Reaching All Learners

Intervention

Draw a strip of five tiles. Color one tile. This represents one out of five. Then add one more strip of five; continue until a pattern is recognized.

Solutions and Samples

12. a. Answers will vary. Accept any solution in which 20% or $\frac{1}{5}$ of the squares are black.

Sample solutions:

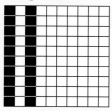 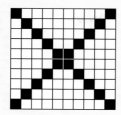

b. Answers will vary depending on individual designs. The chance will be the number of black squares out of the total number of squares. Students might also express this as a fraction.

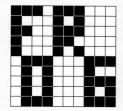 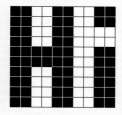

44 black squares

percent: 44%

fraction: $\frac{44}{100}$; $\frac{11}{25}$; $\frac{3}{5}$

ratio: 44 out of 100

or 11 out of 25

60 black squares

percent: 60%

fraction: $\frac{60}{100}$; $\frac{6}{10}$

ratio: 60 out of 100,

6 out of 10, or

3 out of 5

13. You could count the number of black squares and the total number of squares in the floor. The chance of a frog's landing on a black square is the ratio of the black squares to the total number of squares.

Hints and Comments

Materials

black crayons (one per student),
Student Activity Sheet 2 (one per student)

Overview

In the previous problems, students described chances based on the numbers of black and white tiles on given floors. Now they will work backwards by using a given chance to create a tile pattern for a floor. Students also generalize how to find the chance for landing on a black square.

About the Mathematics

Students may use what they learned about ratios and proportions in earlier grades. Several strategies can be used to solve problem 12:

- consecutively coloring one out of every five tiles,
- coloring one row out of every five rows (or two out of every ten rows), or
- computing how many tiles need to be colored before coloring the tiles.

Equivalent ratios are generated with all of these strategies. Some of the equivalent ratios are shown in the ratio table below.

Number of Black Tiles (or Rows)	1	2	20
Total Number of Tiles (or Rows)	5	10	100

This problem may also reinforce students' understanding about the relationship between ratios, fractions, and percents. For example, the ratio one out of five is equivalent to the fraction 1:5 and to 20%.

B What's the Chance?

Notes

14 In this problem, students decide if the spinners can be used to make fair decisions, as was done in Section A. If some students are having difficulty, refer them to that section.

15a Students should be able to use fractions or percents to help them place the spinners on the ladder. Encourage students to express their answer as a ratio, fraction, or percent.

15b If students have difficulty getting started, suggest for spinner i that you are looking for ways to describe the spinner; for example, 50%.

16 This problem makes explicit connections between chances on a spinner and chances on a tile floor.

Spinners

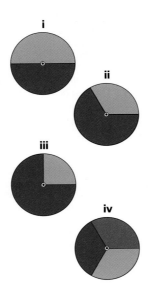

i

ii

iii

iv

14. Study the spinners on the left.

   a. Can you use spinner **i** to make fair decisions? Explain your answer.

   b. Can you use spinner **ii**, **iii**, or **iv** to make fair decisions?

   c. Draw a new spinner—different from **i**, **ii**, **iii**, and **iv**—that can be used to make fair decisions.

15. a. Draw a chance ladder in your notebook. For each spinner on the left, mark the ladder to show the chance of landing in the purple part.

   b. Use a method other than a ladder to express the chance of landing in the purple part of each spinner.

Jim made this spinner and colored this floor. Jim says, "The spinner and the floor give the same chance of landing in the purple part."

16. Do you agree with Jim? Explain.

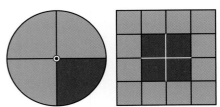

Assessment Pyramid

15a, b

14a–c

Understand the meaning of fair.

Use visual models to estimate chance.

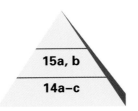

Reaching All Learners

Intervention

Distinguishing parts of a circle and their fractional parts may be very difficult for many students. Make sure that students understand that the fractional parts of the chance ladder should be the same as the fractional parts of the circle.

Advanced Learners

Have students create a floor design that matches each of the spinners.

Solutions and Samples

14. a. Yes, if two people or choices are involved. Since there is an equal chance of landing on either section, the spinner is fair.

b. You cannot use spinners ii and iii to make a fair decision between two people. Spinner iv may be used to make a fair decision with three people.

c. Spinners will vary. Student spinners will probably have sections with equal areas. Sample solutions:

15. a.

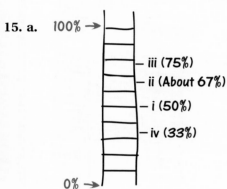

b. Answers will vary. Students may express the chances using percents, ratios, or fractions.

Sample solutions:

i: 50%, one out of two, or $\frac{1}{2}$

ii: about 67%, two out of three, or $\frac{2}{3}$

iii: 75%, three out of four, or $\frac{3}{4}$

iv: about 33%, one out of three, or $\frac{1}{3}$

16. Jim is right. There is a one-out-of-four chance of landing on purple using either the spinner or the tile floor.

Hints and Comments

Overview

Students decide whether or not different spinners can be used to make fair decisions. They represent the chance for landing on the purple part of each spinner with a chance ladder and express the chance as a percent, a fraction, or a ratio. They compare the chance of landing on the purple part of a spinner to the chance of landing on the purple tiles on a floor.

About the Mathematics

Technically, whether or not spinners can be used to make fair decisions depends upon what is being decided. For example, if you want to give outcomes different chances, a spinner with unequal central angles might be considered fair. It is not important to discuss this with students at this time.

Homework

Have student bring chance statements from home to use with problem 17 on the next page.

 **Activity**

B What's the Chance?

Notes

17 The point of the activity is to get a sense of the language of chance in everyday occurrences. If you do this problem in class, be sure to have newspapers available.

17. Look in the newspaper for statements about chance. Put your statements on a chance ladder. Bring the ladder to school and explain why you decided to place statements where you did.

Here are some examples to help you.

Baseball Update
Chances for a Run at Division Title Slim

By Mel Bergman
of The Reporter staff

It was no surprise that the Cal-away CooCoos' manager Regg Loopendorf refused to give a statement regarding his team's

even though the seri led to a new definitio Future chances for a can only hope that it

Dry Spell May End Soon

UPI
Reports that a new attempts to b ival f

...er world that will end all to bri and that will return the focus that

Home Buyer's Guide

THIS MAY BE YOUR LAST CHANCE TO BUY A NEW HOME ON SILVER LAKE

Site rating guide ★★★★

The last 20 homes will go on sale this weekend.

The size and number of families wanting to settle in this spectacular area has increased dramatically over the last few weeks. The few

the range of views and the availability of easy access to many of the recreational outlets bring a new meaning to the term "Land of Dreams"

LATEST LUXURIOUS LISTINGS

Reaching All Learners

Accommodation

Have samples of newspapers available in class for those students who may not have access to a newspaper at home.

Accommodation

Non-readers may want to make a chance ladder and tell a story orally that goes along with their ladder.

English Language Learners

Have students read some of the statements about chance that they found. Discuss any words in the statements that students do not understand.

Solutions and Samples

17. Ladders will vary. Students might find chance statements from advertisements, sports articles, poll results, and so on.

Sample chance ladder:

I think of the 20 homes still on sale, 16 will be sold this weekend. So I positioned this statement at 80% on the chance ladder.

According to the newspaper article that I read, inflation will continue to slowly rise over the next five years. So I positioned this statement at 70% on the chance ladder.

According to the newspaper article that I read, the Chicago Cubs have not played in the World Series for many years. So I positioned this statement at 20% on the chance ladder.

Hints and Comments

Materials

Newspapers and magazines

Overview

Students share with the class chance ladders they constructed to represent newspaper headlines about chance.

Notes

After having a student read the summary aloud, you may wish to have students go back through the section and find problems that support the concepts taught. This will encourage students to actively use the summary section as a study tool.

Be sure to discuss Check Your Work with the students so they understand when to give themselves credit for an answer that is different from the one at the back of the book.

Summary

In this section, you saw different ways of expressing chances. You have seen that the chances on a ladder can be expressed with percents. If it is certain something will happen, you can say the chance is 100%. If it is certain it will not happen, the chance is 0%. Chances can also be expressed with fractions. You can make a chance ladder and label it with fractions instead of percents.

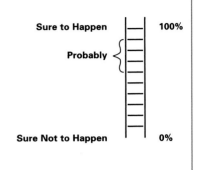

Check Your Work

1. a. What fraction will you use to represent a 50-50 chance?

   b. Put some other fractions where they belong on a chance ladder.

   c. Where will you put a chance of $\frac{1}{6}$ on a chance ladder?

2. Here are some statements about chances. Some of them belong together; they are just different ways of saying the same thing.

On **Student Activity Sheet 3**, connect all statements that say the same thing. One example has already been done.

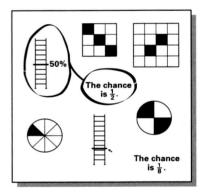

Assessment Pyramid

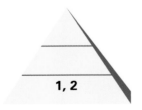

Assesses Section B Goals

Reaching All Learners

Parent Involvement

Have parents review the section with their child to relate the Check Your Work problems to the problems from the section.

Solutions and Samples

Answers to Check Your Work

1. a. $\frac{1}{2}$, or any fraction that is equivalent to it, such as $\frac{5}{10}$ or $\frac{50}{100}$.

b. You may have different answers. Here is one example. Discuss your answer with a classmate and see if you agree with the placement on the ladder.

c. Between 10 and 20%.

2.

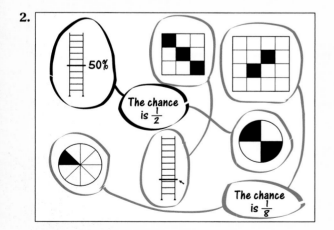

Hints and Comments

Materials

Student Activity Sheet 3 (one per student)

Overview

This page summarizes the main concepts of this section. Different ways of describing chance are tied together: chance ladders, percents, and fractions.

In Check Your Work students assess themselves on the concepts and skills from this section. Students can check their answers on page 38 of the *Take a Chance* Student Book.

Planning

After students complete Section B, you may assign for homework appropriate activities from the Additional Practice section, located on pages 34–36 of the *Take a Chance* Student Book.

Comments About the Solutions

1. a. Some students may still be using the phrase *one out of two*. If so, encourage them to express this as a fraction. Ask them whether or not that ratio is the same as the fraction $\frac{1}{2}$.

b. You may ask your students what fractions belong at "Sure to Happen" and "Sure Not to Happen."

c. You may have students first divide the chance ladder or chance scale in sixths.

2. Some students may need the hint that sometimes more than two statements can be connected.

Notes

For Further Reflection

Reflective questions are meant to summarize and discuss important concepts.

3. Draw a spinner and a tile pattern, each with a black part that represents a chance of 20%.

4. **a.** If your teacher chooses a student's paper to be read in class, what is the chance your paper will be chosen?

   b. How can your teacher do this in a fair way? If your teacher chooses fairly, what is the chance your teacher will choose your paper?

 For Further Reflection

One of your classmates was absent this week. In writing and using drawings, try to explain to the classmate the mathematics that he or she missed this week. Use drawings with your explanation. Make sure to include percents, fractions, and chance ladders.

Assessment Pyramid

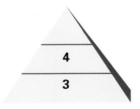

4

3

Assesses Section B Goals

Reaching All Learners

English Language Learners

Bilingual students may want to write the reflection in their native language and share with others who have the same native language.

Solutions and Samples

Answers to Check Your Work, continued.

3. Spinner: $\frac{1}{5}$ should be black and the other $\frac{4}{5}$ another color (you may estimate the $\frac{1}{5}$).

   Tile floor: $\frac{1}{5}$ of the tiles should be black and the rest should be another color (for instance white). It is easy if the floor has a number of tiles that can be divided by 5. So you can make a floor of 25 tiles, 5 of which are black.

4. **a.** If the teacher chooses fairly, the chance will be one out of the number of students in the class. If not, all kinds of other factors could be involved in the chance. For instance, a teacher may choose from only the papers that received an A grade.

   b. The teacher can put all of the students' names in a box and pick one. Then the chance your paper will be chosen is one out of the number of students in your class.

For Further Reflection

Reflective questions are meant to summarize and discuss important concepts.

This question should be discussed in class. Have students display their explanations and drawings.

Hints and Comments

Comments About the Solutions

3. Some students may need to express 20% as a ratio first: this can be "20 out of 100," "2 out of 10," or "1 out of 5." Making the tile floor first may help them to realize that the ratio terminology is helpful. You may refer students back to problem 12 on page 15 if they have difficulty with this problem.

4. The chance can always be expressed in ratio terminology and as the corresponding fraction. Depending on the number of students in the class, it may be more or less difficult to express the chance as a percentage.

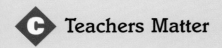

Section Focus

Students predict results, record outcomes, and analyze the results of simple chance experiments. Students develop an informal understanding of the difference between theoretical and experimental chance. The instructional focus of Section C is to:

- **estimate chance from repeated trials of an experiment and**
- **explore theoretical and experimental probability.**

Pacing and Planning

Day 8: Chancy Business		Student pages 20 and 21
INTRODUCTION	Problem 1	Discuss the probable outcome of a chance experiment with a number cube.
ACTIVITY	Problems 2–4	Complete a table of outcomes and make predictions based on the results.
CLASSWORK	Problems 5 and 6	Solve chance problems involving number cubes.
HOMEWORK	Problem 7	Demonstrate knowledge of chance and explain reasoning.

Day 9: Tossing and Turning		Student pages 22 and 23
INTRODUCTION	Problem 8	Identify information from a cumulative data table.
ACTIVITY	Problems 9 and 10	Estimate the theoretical probability of a coin-tossing experiment.
CLASSWORK	Problem 11	Predict the theoretical probability of an outcome in a coin-tossing experiment and then carry out the experiment.
HOMEWORK	Problems 12 and 13	Describe chance situations influenced by personal choice.

Day 10: Find the Chance		Student pages 23 –25
INTRODUCTION	Problem 14	Estimate chance for experiments involving irregularly shaped objects.
CLASSWORK	Check Your Work, Problems 1–5	Student Self-Assessment

Additional Resources: Additional Practice, Section C, Student pages 35 and 36

Materials

Student Resources

Quantities listed are per student.

Teachers' Resources

No resources required.

Student Materials

Quantities listed are per pair of students, unless otherwise noted.

- Student work, Problem 18, Section A, page 6
- Coin
- Number cube

* See Hints and Comments for optional materials.

Learning Lines

Experimental and Theoretical Chance

The concept of chance is further developed. The difference between theoretical and experimental chance is informally addressed. What students expect or predict to happen (theoretical chance) is compared to what actually did happen in the experiment of rolling a number cube (experimental chance). Students experience that by conducting repeated trials of an experiment, like rolling number cubes or tossing a coin, the outcomes will approach the expected outcomes.

Students also realize that when tossing a coin or rolling a number cube, the next outcome is not affected by the previous outcomes. Students estimate or calculate experimental chances as "so many out of so many." This is done in problem 14 based on the outcomes of the activity on page 6 in Section A. In this case no theoretical chances can be found.

Students do not need to know these terms. In the unit *A Second Chance*, more attention is paid to the subject of experimental and theoretical chances.

Variability

By conducting experiments and studying outcomes, students experience that variability will occur in the outcomes. Problem 7 on page 21 is a good problem to discuss this issue.

Models

Students use different types of tables to record results of experiments. A frequency table as well as a cumulative frequency table are used.

The cumulative frequency table can show both the variability of outcomes as well as the fact that the experimental chance approaches the theoretical chance if the number of trials gets bigger. This type of table is used for this purpose in the unit *A Second Chance*.

Mathematical Background to Experimental and Theoretical Chance

Theoretical chance is based on the possible outcomes in a particular experiment and can be determined before the experiment is conducted. Calculating theoretical chance is straightforward when each outcome has an equal chance of occurring. For number cubes, coins, and simple spinners, the theoretical chance can be calculated by dividing the number of selected outcomes by the total number of outcomes. This way of calculating theoretical chances is addressed in the next section. Experimental chance is based on the trials of an experiment and is calculated by dividing the number of times an outcome occurs by the total number of trials. For a large number of trials, experimental chance approximates theoretical chance.

When rolling number cubes and tossing coins, the theoretical chance of each outcome is known. When tossing or rolling irregularly shaped objects, this is not the case. The only way to get insight into the chances for the different outcomes is through repeated trials with each object.

At the End of This Section

Students can estimate chance from repeated trials of an experiment. They know that the experimental chance can be different from what they predicted, but that in the long run for a chance experiment results will get closer and closer to what they expected.

They also know informally that (for independent events) an outcome is not affected by previous outcomes; for example, tossing ten heads in a row does not affect the chance that the next coin toss will be a head. The chance remains 50%.

Notes

Remind students that if a number cube is fair, each number has an equal chance of being rolled.

1 Let students make their own predictions. If they have difficulty, ask them how many times they would expect to roll each of the outcomes 1–6.

3 Ask students to explain why the results of the experiment differed from the expected outcome as determined in problem 1.

4 Predicting outcomes is a key concept in this section. After making predictions, have students investigate what happens.

Let the Good Times Roll

Chancy Business

If you roll a number cube one time, the chance you will roll a 6 is the same as the chance you will roll 5, 4, 3, 2, or 1.

1. If you roll a number cube 30 times, about how many times do you think you will roll a 6?

 Activity

2. Make a table like the one shown below. Roll a number cube 30 times. Tally the number that comes up for each roll.

Number Rolled	Number of Times It Came Up
1	
2	
3	
4	
5	
6	

3. Did what happen differ from what you expected to happen? How?

4. What do you think will happen if you increase the number of rolls to 60?

Reaching All Learners

Vocabulary Building

The word *tally* may be new for some students. As you explain the word, show students how to record their results on the tally chart.

Advanced Learners

As well as tallying the number of times each outcome occurs, have students keep a running total of the sum of all rolls; then use this sum to find the average roll. Have them compare the average to the frequency of each number and make a written comparison of the results.

Solutions and Samples

1. You would expect to roll a 6 about five times.

2. Answers will vary. While on average, each number will come up five times, this will almost never happen in just 30 rolls. Sample student table:

Number Rolled	Number of Times It Came Up
1	||||
2	⊬⊬
3	⊬⊬ |
4	||||
5	⊬⊬ ||||
6	||

3. Answers will vary. With only 30 rolls, some students may have expected that the results would be unbalanced, while other students may have expected that each number would come up five times.

4. Answers will vary, but should suggest that as the number of rolls increases, the results should become more balanced. For example, in 60 rolls, one would expect each number to come up about ten times.

Hints and Comments

Materials

number cubes (one per group of students)

Overview

Students predict the outcome of a chance experiment. They roll a number cube 30 times and tally the results. Then they compare their results to their predictions.

About the Mathematics

Students explore the differences between theoretical chance and experimental chance. Based on theoretical arguments, one can predict the outcomes when rolling a number cube or tossing a coin. But when actually conducting experiments, there may be a lot of variability in the outcomes. The actual outcomes may differ somewhat from theoretical chances.

The problems on this page introduce two important mathematical concepts:

- in independent trials, the next outcome is not affected by previous outcomes, and
- by conducting repeated trials of an experiment, the outcomes will approach the expected outcomes.

Extension

You may want to combine the tables of the whole class and see whether or not the results stabilize. Discuss the results with the class. With more data, the actual outcome of each number should come closer to expected theoretical outcomes than the results of any one table.

Let the Good Times Roll

Notes

5a Make sure students realize that counting tallies is easier if they count first by fives or by tens, and then count the single tallies.

5b It may help to state that on each roll, the number cube does not remember what happened before, so the chances for each outcome remain unchanged.

6 This problem works well in small groups, but be sure to discuss expected results versus actual events with the whole class.

7 Since this is a crucial problem and can be used for reflection, it should be discussed in class. It focuses on the fact that outcomes tend to approach theoretical probabilities after repeated trials. In this case, each outcome will occur about the same number of times.

Nina rolled a number cube. She recorded the results in a table.

Number Rolled	Number of Times It Came Up
1	///
2	7HL 7HL /
3	7HL 7HL
4	7HL 7HL /
5	7HL ///
6	7HL 7HL ///

5. a. How many times did Nina roll the number cube?

b. Nina says, "The chance of rolling 1 on the next roll is greater than the chance of rolling 6." Do you think she is right?

6. a. Robert rolled a number cube six times. Do you think he rolled a 4? Explain.

b. Then Robert rolled the number cube 20 times more. Do you think he rolled a 4 this time?

Now We're Rolling!

Hillary rolled a number cube many times as part of an experiment.

7. Unfortunately, Hillary's pen leaked and covered up the number of times 6 came up. What do you think is written under the spill? Explain.

Number Rolled	1	2	3	4	5
Number of Times It Came Up	44	36	37	41	39

Assessment Pyramid

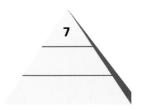

Understand the meaning of chance (variability)

Reaching All Learners

Intervention

Students should actually roll the number cube and count the results after four rolls and after 20 rolls, and then compare the results. The important mathematics here is that the students understand that more rolls lead to more chances of a particular number appearing as a result.

Solutions and Samples

5. a. Nina rolled the number cube 56 times.

   b. Nina is wrong. Even though she did not get as many ones as she had expected, that does not affect the chance of rolling a 1 on the next roll.

6. a. Answers will vary. Possible response:

      You can't be sure that Robert rolled a 4, since he rolled the number cube only six times.

   b. Answers will vary. In this case, it is almost certain he has thrown a 4 but, again, not absolutely certain.

7. Answers will vary. However, since the rolls for the other numbers ranged from 36 to 44, it is reasonable to expect the number of 6's also to be in the high 30s or low 40s. The number of 6's could be outside this range, however.

Hints and Comments

Overview

Students solve more chance problems involving number cubes and reason about the possible outcomes.

About the Mathematics

Students reason about theoretical chances compared to experimental chances in problems using number cubes. Problems 5 and 6 focus on the fact that the outcome of each roll is independent of the outcomes of previous rolls. Problem 7 deals with variability in the results of a chance experiment.

Planning

Students should realize that the outcome of each roll is not affected by outcomes on previous rolls. You may want to have them continue to experiment with rolling a number cube to see that this is actually so.

Comments About the Solutions

   5. b. This may be a challenging problem for some students. Looking at the table, they may erroneously reason that since so few 1's have been rolled so far, there is a greater chance of rolling a 1.

Let the Good Times Roll

Notes

10 This is a reflective problem. Before students answer this problem, ask them how to estimate the percent of heads for each row in the table.

11 Make sure students understand how to fill in the table. This problem is critical since it shows that experimental outcomes tend to approach theoretical ones with repeated trials.

11c You may want to do this problem as a whole class activity.

After students finish problem 11, you might have a short class discussion about the fact that experimental outcomes tend to approach theoretical ones with repeated trials but that variability will always occur within the results.

Tossing and Turning

During World War II, English mathematician John Kerrich was locked in a cell. He had a coin with him and decided to do an experiment to pass the time. While in the cell, he tossed the coin 10,000 times and recorded the results.

Here is the start of a chart he might have made.

8. a. Did the first toss come up heads?

b. On which toss did the mathematician get heads for the first time?

c. How many tosses did it take to get three heads?

d. How many tails had come up after eight tosses?

9. About how many heads do you think had come up after 10,000 tosses?

Number of Tosses	Total Number of Heads
1	0
2	0
3	1
4	1
5	2
6	2
7	3
8	3
9	4

10. Reflect How does the percent of heads change as the number of coin tosses increases?

Activity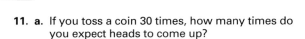

11. a. If you toss a coin 30 times, how many times do you expect heads to come up?

Toss a coin 30 times. Tally the results in a table like the one on the right.

b. Did your results match what you predicted?

c. Combine your results with those of everyone in the class. How do the class results compare to your individual results?

H	T

Reaching All Learners

Intervention

Make a chart like the one on this page and toss a coin nine times. Record the total number of heads rolled after each toss. Then discuss the chart and what the results show.

Advanced Learners

Students may add a third column on the chart that indicates the percent of heads after each roll. Have them then predict what would happen after 50 rolls, 100 rolls, etc. The percent should approach 50% as the number of rolls increases. You may even want to have students graph the results of number of rolls versus percents.

Solutions and Samples

8. a. No.

    b. On the third toss.

    c. Seven tosses.

    d. Five tails.

9. About 5,000 heads.

10. The percent of heads should approach 50% as the number of coin tosses increases.

11. a. Heads should come up about 15 times.

    b. Answers will vary. It is quite unlikely that every student will get exactly 15 heads and 15 tails. However, students' actual results should be close to these expected results.

    c. Students should notice that the class results are more in line with the expected results of a 50-50 chance of heads or tails coming up.

Hints and Comments

Materials

coins (one per group of students)

Overview

Students investigate the differences between theoretical and experimental chances within the context of tossing a coin.

About the Mathematics

Although the mathematical concepts dealt with on this page are essentially the same as with the number cube, the context of tossing a coin is different. In a coin toss, the two outcomes are equally likely to occur. The chances are expressed using percents. Since the chances of tossing a head or a tail are each 1:2 or 50%, students should have few problems working with percent. The table in problem 8 differs from other tables used in this section. It is a cumulative table, which shows the total number of heads over time. On each roll, the total number of heads either stays the same or increases by one. By comparing the total number of heads to the total number of rolls, the percent of heads can be estimated or calculated. The percent of heads occurring approaches 50% as the number of rolls increases.

Let the Good Times Roll

Notes

Have a student read this text aloud. It is critical for students' understanding of experimental and theoretical outcomes of repeated trials.

12b Put a table on the overhead projector or board that students can put their results in as they complete this activity.

13 Students' explanations are more important than their answers.

14 Discuss each group's answers with the whole class. Listen for students' understanding of fractions, percents, and ratios.

As you toss a coin many times, the percent of heads approaches 50%, or $\frac{1}{2}$. We say the chance of getting heads is $\frac{1}{2}$.

On any single toss, though, you cannot tell whether heads or tails will come up. Although you cannot predict a single event with certainty, if you repeat an experiment many times, a pattern may appear.

Think B4 You Act

Pick a number from 1 to 4 and write it on a piece of paper.

12. a. If every student in the class writes down one number, how many times do you expect each number to be picked?

b. Count all the 1s, 2s, 3s, and 4s selected and put the information in a table. Study the results. Is this what you expected? Why or why not?

13. Reflect If you were a game show host and were putting a prize behind one of four doors, where would you put the prize? Give a reason for your choice.

Find the Chance

In problem 18 on page 6, you experimented with these objects:

- A large paper cup
- A small paper cup
- A chalkboard eraser
- A bottle cap
- A spinner like the one on the left

14. Look again at problem 18 on page 6. Based on the 30 tosses or spins for your object, estimate the chance of each outcome.

Assessment Pyramid

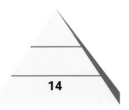

14

Express chance for situations using percents, fractions, and ratios.

Reaching All Learners

Accommodation

Make a chart for the class that includes fractions, decimals, and percents for the number of outcomes based on problem 18 on page 6. Students may use the chart to match their own results.

Vocabulary

Make sure students understand that a trial is one of many repetitions of an experiment. They could put examples in the vocabulary section of their student notebooks.

Solutions and Samples

12. a. Answers will vary. You would expect all the numbers to have an equal chance, but 3 tends to be picked most often, followed by 2, then 1 or 4.

  b. Answers will vary. The results are probably not what students expected because "random" number picks are not really random, since people tend not to pick the numbers on either end of a given range.

13. A game show host should put the prize where the chance of its being picked is lowest, either behind door one or door four.

14. Some rough estimates are as follows:

a.

Large Cup Toss	
Top	5%
Side	90%
Bottom	5%

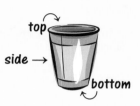

b.

Small Cup Toss	
Top	5%
Side	90%
Bottom	5%

c.

Eraser Toss	
Top	45%
Side	5%
Bottom	45%
Side	5%

d.

Cap Toss	
Top	50%
Bottom	50%

e.

Spinner	
Purple	50%
Green	50%

Hints and Comments

Materials

Students' work from problem 18 on page 6 of the Student Book.

Overview

The three main concepts dealt with in this section are summarized here. Students discover that outcomes of chance experiments do not always approach theoretical possibilities. This may be due to psychological factors. Students estimate chances based on the results of the experiment they conducted with irregularly shaped objects in Section A.

About the Mathematics

Students experiment with picking a number from one to four; the chances seem to be predictable, based on theoretical considerations. Each number has the same chance of being picked only if the numbers are randomly chosen. Many people have preferences for certain numbers and tend to avoid extremes (one and four), so people do not choose numbers randomly. So, in this case, the experimental outcomes, even when repeated many times, are not likely to approach theoretical outcomes. When rolling number cubes and tossing coins, the theoretical chance of each outcome is known. When tossing or rolling irregularly shaped objects, this is not the case. The only way to get insight into the chances for the different outcomes is through repeated trials with each object. It is important that students discover that:

- outcomes are not equally likely in all chance experiments,
- you cannot always predict outcomes, and
- an experiment may give insight into the chance distribution.

Planning

Students need to complete problem 18 on page 6 before doing problem 14.

Comments About the Solutions

13. Some students may reason from the viewpoint of the contestant, rather than the game show host, and put the prize behind the door with their favorite number.

14. It is not necessary for students to calculate exact chances here. If students have difficulty, ask them to first order the outcomes from least to most likely. They can express the chances using a ratio; for example, *The chances are so many times out of 30.*

Let the Good Times Roll

Notes

After having a student read the summary aloud, you may wish to have them go back through the section and find problems that support the concepts taught. This will encourage students to actively use the summary section as a study tool.

Be sure to discuss Check Your Work with your students so they understand when to give themselves credit for an answer that is different from the one at the back of the book.

Let the Good Times Roll

Summary

You can find the chance of an event by experimenting with many, many trials. In the short run, what happens may not be what you expect. But in the long run, your results will get closer and closer to what you expect.

When you are tossing a coin or rolling a number cube, each new **trial** will offer the same chances as the previous one. A coin or number cube cannot "remember" what side it landed on last.

Check Your Work

1. **a.** If you toss a coin 10 times and get heads every time, what is the chance of getting heads on the 11th toss?
   b. If you roll a number cube over and over again, what do you think will happen to the percent of even numbers that come up?

Suppose you were to toss a fair coin 100 times.

2. **a.** About how many heads would you expect to get?
   b. Would it be reasonable to get 46 heads? Why or why not?

Robert and his classmates are going to roll a number cube 500 times and record their results in a table.

3. Predict their results by filling in the second row of the table with numbers you think are likely for Robert's class. Then explain why you filled in the numbers the way you did.

Number Rolled	1	2	3	4	5	6
Number of Times It Came Up						

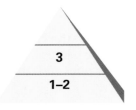

Assessment Pyramid

3

1–2

Assess Section C goals

Reaching All Learners

Parent Involvement

Have students ask their parents for an old coin. Have them toss this coin and see if the results differ. Discuss why this may be the case.

Vocabulary

Make sure students understand that a trial is one of many repetitions of an experiment. They could put examples in the vocabulary section of their student notebooks.

24 Take a Chance

Solutions and Samples

Answers to Check Your Work

1. a. 50% or $\frac{1}{2}$. Each flip of the coin is independent of the flips before.

   b. The percent of even numbers will probably get closer to 50%.

2. a. You would expect to get heads about half of the time, or 50 heads.

   b. It would be reasonable, because you don't always get exactly what you expect. Your results should be close to your expectations, though, and 46 is pretty close to 50.

3. Different answers are possible. The number of times each number is rolled should be about the same because each number has the same chance of coming up. In the long run, each number should come up in about $\frac{1}{6}$ of the rolls. So the results for each number should be close to $\frac{500}{6}$, which is about 83. Be sure to use 500 as the total number of rolls in your calculations. A possible answer follows:

Number Rolled	1	2	3	4	5	6
Number of Times It Came Up	80	78	90	85	76	91

Hints and Comments

Overview

Students read the Summary and make predictions about experiments involving coins and number cubes. In Check Your Work students assess themselves on the concepts and skills from this section. Students can check their answers on page 39 of the *Take a Chance* Student Book.

Planning

After students complete Section C, you may assign for homework appropriate activities from the Additional Practice section, located on pages 34–36 of the *Take a Chance* Student Book.

Comments About the Solutions

1. b. If students are having difficulty, ask H*ow many even and odd numbers does a number cube have?* (three even numbers and three odd numbers) *What do you think will happen to the percent of even numbers after repeated trials?* (After repeated trials, the outcomes for even numbers should be about equal to those of odd numbers.) You might also let students roll a number cube many times and tally their results.

2. If students are having difficulty, have them look back at previous problems involving tossing a coin. For b there will always be variability in the results even after repeated trials.

3. Make sure that students see the numbers as being in a range and avoid having students focus on the one good answer. Due to variability a "one good answer" does not exist. This problem is comparable to problem 7 on page 21 of the student book.

4. a. Design a three-color spinner that is not fair. Spin it 30 times and record the results.

   b. Based on the 30 spins, estimate the chance for each color.

Robert made a four-color spinner. After 50 spins, he recorded the following results.

Red	12
Blue	24
Green	6
Purple	8

5. a. Draw what his spinner may have looked like.

   b. If you used the spinner you drew 50 times, would the results be exactly the same as in the table? Why or why not?

For Further Reflection

Reflective questions are meant to summarize and discuss important concepts.

For Further Reflection

"If you toss a coin 6 times and you get heads every time, then it is more likely that tails will come up on the next roll." Is this statement true or false? Why or why not?

Assessment Pyramid

4, 5

☐ FFR

Assess Section C Goals

Reaching All Learners

Accommodation

Provide circles for spinners.

Solutions and Samples

4. a. Discuss your answers with a classmate. The colored sections must be different in size. If the difference is great enough, it will affect the results of the spins.

b. Use the number of times out of 30 spins that the spinner landed on each color to estimate the chance for that color. You may write this as a percent. If this is difficult for you, look at problem 14.

5. a. Spinner must be about half (50%) blue, a quarter (25%) red, one-eighth (half a quarter, or 12.5%) green, and one-eighth purple.

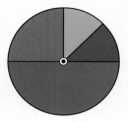

b. The results probably wouldn't be exactly the same, but close. Since 50 spins is not very many, the results may differ a little from what you expect. If you do not feel sure, make the spinner and spin it 50 times.

For Further Reflection

Reflective questions are meant to summarize and discuss important concepts.

The statement is false. The coin does not "remember" previous tosses, so the chance tails will come up is still $\frac{1}{2}$ or 50%.

Hints and Comments

Comments About the Problems

4. a. The angles of the sections on the spinner must be unequal in order to have an unfair spinner. It is not necessary that each of the three colors is used only once, although most students will probably do this.

b. Students may give the chance as a ratio. This problem is related to problem 14 on page 23.

5. In this problem students reason from the results to make the appropriate spinner. It is the reverse from problem 4.

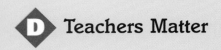
Section Focus

Students explore chance situations involving multiple events and determine possible outcomes using tree diagrams and tables. The instructional focus of Section D is to:

- **determine all combinations and possible outcomes using tree diagrams and tables;**
- **simulate simple events by using coins and number cubes to estimate or check the chances for possible outcomes; and**
- **calculate chance for simple situations involving multiple events by counting possibilities.**

Pacing and Planning

Day 11: Families		Student pages 26, 27, 32
INTRODUCTION	Problem 1 and 2	Estimate chance by determining possible outcomes.
CLASSWORK	Problems 3–8	Use tree diagrams to identify and record the possible combination of shirts and pants.
HOMEWORK	Check Your Work, Problems 1–2	Student Self-Assessment: Use a tree diagram to represent combinations.

Day 12: Two Children Again		Student pages 28 and 29
INTRODUCTION	Problem 9	Discuss the use of tree diagrams to describe the chance of families having a boy or a girl.
CLASSWORK	Problems 10 and 11	Use tree diagrams to investigate the possible combinations of boys and girls in one-, two-, and three-child families.
HOMEWORK	Problems 12–14	Determine all the possible outcomes in a game.

Day 13: Sum It Up		Student pages 29 and 30
ACTIVITY	Problems 15–19	Predict and calculate the likelihood of possible outcomes of a game involving number cubes.
HOMEWORK	Problems 20–22	Complete charts and tree diagrams to show all possible combinations resulting from rolling two number cubes.

Day 14: Treasure		Student pages 31–33
INTRODUCTION	Problem 23	From information given in a riddle, identify paths and combinations of paths for coin flip results.
CLASSWORK	Problems 24 and 25 Discuss Summary	Locate an area on a checkerboard that identifies the location of a buried treasure.
HOMEWORK	Check Your Work, Problems 3–5	Student Self-Assessment

Additional Resources: Additional Practice, Section D, Student page 36

Materials

Student Resources

Quantities listed are per pair of students, unless otherwise noted.

• Student Activity Sheet 4

Teachers' Resources

No resources required.

Student Materials

• Different colored number cubes, two
• Pennies, two

*See Hints and Comments for optional materials.

Learning Lines

Possible Outcomes

In this section students use a variety of methods to represent and count the possible outcomes in different multi-event situations. At first students can use their own way to show all possible outcomes. They can for example use drawings, lists, diagrams. Later the tree diagram and a "table" are introduced as a way to do this.

Chance in Multi-Event Situations

Students first predict the theoretical chance in a multi-event situation, represented in a tree diagram. The context is the possible combination of boys and girls in families with two or more children. Students use a simulation with coins to find the experimental chance.

After finding all possible outcomes, students can find the chances on any outcome as the ratio of the number of favorable outcomes out of all the possible outcomes. This idea was addressed informally in Section B in the context of the tiled floor. Here it is revisited in a preformal way in problems 19 and 20 on page 30. A formal chance definition based on this way of finding chances is introduced in the unit *A Second Chance.*

The idea of complementary chances is informally addressed. Here, for example, students are asked to find the chance of 'not rolling a sum of 10 with two number cubes.' This is revisited in the unit *A Second Chance.*

Models

The tree diagram, which was introduced in Section B, is extended to represent combined events, like choosing a T-shirt and choosing a pair of pants or having a first child and having a second child or the way Hillary holds her hand and the way Robert holds his. Students use tree diagrams to represent and determine the likelihood of possible combinations. By tracing the paths along the branches, students can find all favorable and all possible outcomes. A grid or table is also used to show and count all possible outcomes and find chances.

At the End of This Section

Students can list and count all possible outcomes in multi-event situations involving two or three combined events by using tree diagrams or other methods. They can determine the chance a single outcome will occur by finding the ratio of the number of favorable outcomes to all possible outcomes.

Let Me Count the Ways

Families

There are many different types of families.

Some families have one adult.

Some families have two adults, and some families have more.

Some families have children, and some do not.

1b You might want to initially discuss this problem with students to help clarify their reasoning. It is not important that all students be convinced of any particular answer at this point, since this topic is revisited on page 28 of the Student Book.

2 Be sure to discuss this problem in class. It is critical because it introduces simulation.

1. **a.** Suppose you look at 20 families with two children. How many of these families do you think will have one boy and one girl?

   b. Other students in your class may not agree with your answer to part **a**. Explain why you think your answer is the most likely. Drawing a diagram may be helpful.

2. You can simulate a study of two-child families by tossing two pennies. Heads will represent a girl, and tails will represent a boy. Toss the two pennies 20 times. See how many families with one boy and one girl you get. Was the result the same as your guess for problem 1a?

 girl

 boy

Assessment Pyramid

Use repeated trials to estimate chance.

Reaching All Learners

Advanced Learners

Some students may question whether tossing two coins at one time is the same as tossing one coin two times. Have them try the simulation both ways and compare the results.

Intervention

Draw a chart on the board or overhead that shows students how to record the heads/tails tosses. Then show them how to count the pairs and to record their results.

Solutions and Samples

1. a. Answers will vary. Accept any answer that is supported by logical reasoning in part b.

Possible answer: About ten families will have one boy and one girl.

b. Sample answer explanation:

There are four different outcomes; two out of the four outcomes give one boy and one girl. So half of the families will probably have one boy and one girl.

First Child	Second Child
boy	girl
boy	boy
girl	boy
girl	girl

Sample incorrect answer explanation:

You can have one boy and one girl, two boys, or two girls. So about one-third, or seven of the 20 families, will have one boy and one girl.

1B and 1G

2B

2G

2. Answers will vary. Possible distribution of tosses: two heads, five times; two tails, five times; one head and one tail, ten times.

Hints and Comments

Materials

pennies (two per student or small group of students)

Overview

Students list the possible combinations of boys and girls in two-child families and predict how many two-child families out of 20 they think would have one boy and one girl. After explaining their predictions, students simulate the same situation by tossing two coins.

About the Mathematics

Students reason about two child families. They first think about how many families out of 20 expect to have a boy and a girl. There are four possibilities BB, BG, GB, and GG and not three as some students may assume. To understand this better, a simulation is used. Students compare the results of what they think to the results of the simulation.

Comments About the Solutions

1. a. Some students may incorrectly reason that 1:3 of the families will have one boy and one girl (since there are three possible outcomes). However, there are actually four possible outcomes for two children: boy-boy, boy-girl, girl-boy, and girl-girl. Since boy-girl and girl-boy each result in a family with one boy and one girl, their combined chance is 2:4 or 1:2.

Let Me Count the Ways

Notes

Students may need to draw many combinations before they discover that the number of pants times the number of shirts equals the number of possibilities.

6 Encourage students to study the different shirts and pants pictured.

8 Problem 8 provides an excellent opportunity for students to show multiple strategies to solve a problem. Have students share their strategies.

Robert's Clothes

Here are Robert's clothes.

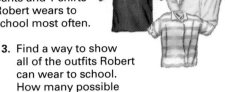
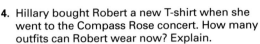
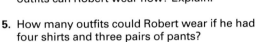

Here are the pants and T-shirts Robert wears to school most often.

3. Find a way to show all of the outfits Robert can wear to school. How many possible outfits are there?

4. Hillary bought Robert a new T-shirt when she went to the Compass Rose concert. How many outfits can Robert wear now? Explain.

5. How many outfits could Robert wear if he had four shirts and three pairs of pants?

Hillary's Clothes

One day, Hillary chooses her shirt and pants with her eyes closed.

6. What outfit do you expect to see Hillary wearing?

7. How could Hillary have used number cubes to help her choose her clothes?

8. Hillary says, "The chance I will pick my star shirt and plaid pants is 1 out of 36." Is Hillary right? Explain.

Reaching All Learners

Intervention

For problem number 7, have students use two number cubes and spend some time tossing the cubes and recording the results in a table. Then they can fill in the missing combinations. Make the connection between the number cubes and the number of shirts and pants.

Accommodation

Provide cut-out shirts and pants so students can manipulate the various combinations and then record the possibilities. Non-readers may paste the different outfits onto a notebook page.

Solutions and Samples

3. There are six different outfits that Robert can wear.

pants   shirts
  2   3

so there are 2 x 3 = 6 possibilities

4. There are eight possible outfits. Explanations may vary. Sample explanation: The new shirt can be worn with either pair of pants, making a total of two new outfits. Adding the two new outfits to the six outfits Robert already has makes a total of eight different outfits.

5. 12 different outfits

6. Hillary will most likely wear a white shirt and green pants because there are more white shirts and green pants in her wardrobe than anything else.

7. Assign each of the six shirts to one of the six numbers on one number cube and each of the six pants to one of the six numbers on a different number cube. A single roll of both cubes will result in one outfit.

8. Yes. There are 36 different outfits she can wear if all T-shirts and all pants are different. The star shirt and the plaid pants together are one of the 36 outfits.

Hints and Comments

Materials

Copies or an overhead transparency of the clothes shown on page 27 of the Student Book, optional.

Overview

Students find efficient ways to record the total number of possible outfits that can be made from sets of shirts and pairs of pants. They predict which outfit is most likely if clothes are picked by chance.

About the Mathematics

The answers are presented in an informal tree diagram. This can be helpful for finding the total number of possible combinations. Multiplying the number of pants by the number of shirts to find this total illustrates an important concept that is developed in this section. Using the tree diagram will help students understand this concept. A chart or table is another helpful method in which to record the possible combinations in a systematic way.

Comments About the Solutions

3. Students may use a variety of strategies:
- make drawings of all possible outfits,
- cut out the clothes and show all the outfits, and
- record the outfits in a chart.

5. Some students may be able to find this by generalizing from their results in problems 3 and 4.

6. Encourage students to study the different shirts and pants pictured. Since there are three similar shirts, outfits with this shirt are most likely.

8. It is important that students are able to explain where the number 36 comes from. (There are a total of 36 possible outfits.) Discuss students' strategies. Some students may need to draw a tree diagram, while others may make a table or a list. Some may reason that for each pair of pants, there are six different T-shirts. There are six pairs of pants, making a total of 36 possibilities (some of which look the same). Since drawing is time consuming, some students may use shortcuts, with colors, letters, or numbers representing the different shirts and pants.

◆ D Let Me Count the Ways

Notes

9 Encourage students to answer in ratios, fractions, and percents.

10d Discuss students' answers to this problem to make sure they understand how to read a tree diagram. Make sure students understand that the order does not matter.

11 Struggling students may need help understanding that each row on the tree diagram represents a new child.

Two Children Again

Tree diagrams can be useful for smart counting and solving problems about chance.

Consider families with children once more.

A tree diagram can show the two possibilities for one child.

9. Each path on this tree diagram represents an equal chance. What is the chance of having a girl?

If a family has a second child, you can extend the tree diagram like this one.

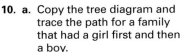

10. a. Copy the tree diagram and trace the path for a family that had a girl first and then a boy.

b. What are all the possible combinations for a family with two children?

c. If there were 20 families with two children in Hillary's class, about how many would you expect to have two girls? What is the chance a family would have two girls?

d. Is the chance greater of having two girls or of having a boy and a girl? Explain.

Now consider families that have three children.

11. a. Extend the tree diagram to show a third child.

b. List all of the different possibilities for a family with three children.

c. Robert says, "It's less likely for a family to have three girls than to have two girls and a boy." Explain this statement.

d. Use the tree diagram from part **a** to make some other statements.

Reaching All Learners

Intervention

Children may have difficulty counting since they need to count GB as one possibility and BG as a different possibility. Students who count GB and BG as the same thing will then have only three outcomes for two children and will have the wrong chance statements. Help them to count the possibilities and make sure they know how to count extended tree diagrams.

Vocabulary

Have students add the vocabulary word *combinations* to their student notebooks. The term *combinations* refers to the birth order for one boy and one girl.

Solutions and Samples

9. one out of two, $\frac{1}{2}$, or 50%

10. a.

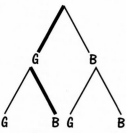

b. BG, GB, BB, and GG

c. about five, which is equivalent to one out of four, or $\frac{1}{4}$ of the families

d. A family has a better chance of having a boy and a girl than two girls, since the chance of having a boy and a girl is $\frac{1}{2}$, and the chance of having two girls is $\frac{1}{4}$. One-half is greater than one-fourth.

11. a.

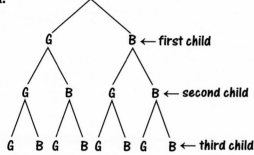

b.

BBB	GBB
BBG	GBG
BGB	GGB
BGG	GGG

c. There is only a $\frac{1}{8}$ or one out of eight chance of getting three girls. There is a $\frac{3}{8}$ or three out of eight chance of getting two girls and one boy.

d. Answers will vary. Sample responses:

- The chance of having two boys and one girl is the same as the chance of having two girls and one boy.

- The chance of having three boys is the same as the chance of having three girls.

- The chance of having three boys is less than the chance of having one boy and two girls.

Hints and Comments

Overview

Students use tree diagrams to investigate the possible combinations of boys and girls in one-, two-, and three-child families.

About the Mathematics

Tree diagrams are again used to represent all possible outcomes. To find all possible combinations of boys and girls from these tree diagrams, one has to carefully trace each path. At each intersection, a boy or a girl is chosen. Different paths can lead to the same combination of boys and girls but in a different order. In some situations, order is important; in others it is not.

Planning

After problem 10b, discuss how students can find all the combinations from the tree diagram by tracing each path and writing down each letter they pass. You may also want to discuss situations in which the order of the letters in each path is important and situations in which it is not. For example, in problem 10a, the order is important, while in problems 10c and 10d, it is not.

Comments About the Solutions

10. c. You may have students label each branch with a number of families.

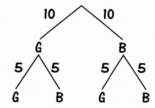

D Let Me Count the Ways

Notes

12 Do this problem with the class to ensure understanding.

13 Struggling students may need to continue the table using O or C to represent Open and Closed.

14 Make sure students explain their reasoning in terms of chance and probability.

15 You may have students list all possible rolls with two number cubes and then find the sums.

Open or Closed?

For a group of three people, here is a way of choosing one person.

Stand in a circle, facing one another. One of you (or everyone at once) says, "One, two, three…go!" At "Go," each person puts out either an open hand or a closed fist.

Hillary, Robert, and Kevin played the game. Each winner is shown on the right in the table below.

Hillary	Robert	Kevin	Winner
			Robert
			Hillary
			No Winner

12. Name another situation in which there is no winner with this method.

13. How many combinations of open and closed hands are possible in the game? List as many as you can. You can use a tree diagram.

14. Do you think this is a fair way to decide something? Explain.

Activity

Sum It Up

15. Roll two different-color number cubes. Using all of the pairs of numbers that can come up, what are the different sums you can get?

Hillary and Robert sometimes play Sum It Up during lunch.

Assessment Pyramid

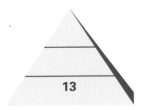

Determine all combinations and possible outcomes.

Reaching All Learners

Act It Out

Students actually play the game and record results.

Advanced Learners

Have students predict what would happen if more than three people play the game. Then have them draw a table that lists all possible results, including ties.

Solutions and Samples

12. Three closed fists will produce no winner, since the winner is the person whose hand does not match the others' hands.

13. There are eight possibilities:

Hillary	Robert	Kevin	Winner
open	open	open	none
open	open	closed	Kevin
open	closed	open	Robert
open	closed	closed	Hillary
closed	open	open	Hillary
closed	open	closed	Robert
closed	closed	open	Kevin
closed	closed	closed	none

14. Yes, this method is fair. There is a total of eight possible outcomes, and each person can win two ways—if his or her hand is open and the other two hands are closed, and if his or her hand is closed and the other two hands are open. So each person has a two out of eight (or one out of four) chance of winning.

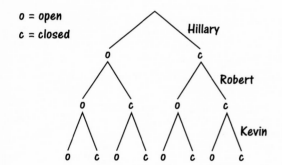

15. You can roll sums from 2 to 12.

Hints and Comments

Materials

colored number cubes (two different-colored cubes per pair of students)

Overview

In a game situation using open hands and closed fists, students determine all the possible outcomes and decide whether or not the game is fair.

Students determine all possible sums that can be obtained when tossing two number cubes.

About the Mathematics

To decide whether or not the "open or closed" game is a fair game, the number of favorable outcomes must be compared with the total number of possible outcomes. Listing all possible combinations in a systematic way is important to ensure that no possible outcome is accidentally omitted. When students look at all possible outcomes, it becomes clear that each of the three players has an equal chance of winning; that is, for each player, two out of the eight possible outcomes are favorable. This is a stepping stone for a chance definition, introduced in the unit *A Second Chance*. For the two number cubes students must also list possible outcomes in a systematic way to find all possible sums.

Comments About the Solutions

13. Students should realize that there are actually three situations here in which a choice has to be made: one for Kevin, one for Robert, and one for Hillary. Each person has two choices (open or closed fist), so there are eight total possibilities. Since this game has two possible outcomes, with an equal chance for each person (open or closed), the game can be simulated with coins, like the two child situation. Be aware that the game, as it is presented here, is only fair when played by three people.

16 At this point, many students may have no idea which sum is best to pick. Encourage them to make a guess.

18 Students who don't recognize that 7 is the best sum, may realize this after problem 19d.

19 You might want to discuss how the different sums from the grid come from the number cubes.

20 Ask students to explain how the total number of outcomes and the different sums can be located in the tree diagram.

They each pick one of the possible sums of two number cubes. Then they roll the number cubes, and the first person to roll his or her sum four times wins. The loser has to clean up the winner's lunch table.

16. Which sum do you think will be best to pick?

Play the game with another person. If you both want the same number, come up with a fair way to decide who gets the number. Record the sums.

17. What was the winning sum in your game?

Play the game five or six times. Change numbers if you want.

18. Now what do you think is the best sum to choose?

19. Student Activity Sheet 4 has a grid showing the possible numbers for each of two number cubes.

Grid with rows labeled 6, 5, 4, 3, 2, 1 and columns labeled 1, 2, 3, 4, 5, 6.

 a. For each square, fill in the sum of the numbers.

 b. How many different combinations are possible when you roll two number cubes?

 c. How many ways can you get a sum of 10 with two number cubes?

 d. What is the best number to pick if you are playing Sum It Up? Is your answer different from your choice in problem 18 above?

20. a. Draw a tree diagram to show all of the possible combinations for rolling two number cubes. It might be messy!

 b. Color the squares in the grid from problem 19 and the paths in the tree diagram from part **a** that give the sum of 10.

 c. What is the chance of rolling the sum of 10?

21. a. What is the chance of rolling two 1s? What is the chance of rolling doubles?

 b. What is the chance of rolling 7?

22. What do you think is the chance of *not* getting 10? *Not* getting 7?

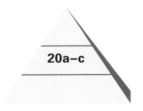
Reaching All Learners

Advanced Learners

Have students find all possible patterns in this grid and then make probability statements about the patterns. Ask: *How many times is the sum odd? How many times is the sum even?*

Extension

Have students complete the same grid but for products of the numbers. This helps to review basic multiplication facts. Then compare the number of different outcomes. Ask: *How many products are even? How many products are odd?*

Solutions and Samples

16. Answers will vary. Actually, seven is the best choice. Seven has the highest probability of being rolled because there are the greatest number of ways to roll a sum of seven.

17. Answers will vary.

18. Seven is the best sum to choose.

19. a.

	1	**2**	**3**	**4**	**5**	**6**
1	2	3	4	5	6	7
2	3	4	5	6	7	8
3	4	5	6	7	8	9
4	5	6	7	8	9	10
5	6	7	8	9	10	11
6	7	8	9	10	11	12

b. 36 combinations.

c. A sum of 10 can be thrown three different ways: 6 + 4, 4 + 6, and 5 + 5.

d. Seven. Answers will vary, depending on the sum students chose in problem 18.

20. a.

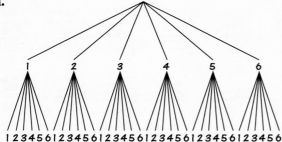

b.

	1	**2**	**3**	**4**	**5**	**6**
6	2	3	4	5	6	7
5	3	4	5	6	7	8
4	4	5	6	7	8	9
3	5	6	7	8	9	10
2	6	7	8	9	10	11
1	7	8	9	10	11	12

c. The chance of rolling the sum of 10 is 3 out of 36, or $\frac{3}{36} = \frac{1}{12}$.

21. a. The chance of rolling two ones is 1 out of 36.

The chance of rolling doubles is 6 out of 36 or one out of six or $\frac{1}{6}$.

b. The chance of rolling a 7 is 6 out of 36.

Hints and Comments

Materials

two different-colored number cubes per pair of students; Student Activity Sheet 4 (one per student)

Overview

Students play the game "Sum It Up" with a partner. The rules are described in the activity on page 30. Based on the experiment, students decide which of the possible sums is the "best" to choose. The theory behind the game is investigated. Students fill in charts and draw tree diagrams to show the possible outcomes for rolling two number cubes. They investigate the chances of different outcomes.

About the Mathematics

Students again investigate the differences between experimental and theoretical chances. Since students have had more practice with listing the possible outcomes of multi-event situations, they can now understand the theory behind predicting the outcomes of rolling two number cubes. They investigate this two-event situation using a chart and a tree diagram.

Planning

Ask students to list the outcomes of the activity. While discussing the answers to problem 18, you do not need to discuss explanations or go into the methods for finding them. Students will do that in the next problems.

Comments About the Solutions

17. Initially, some pairs of students may each pick a number that does not come up often.

19. You might discuss how the different sums from the grid come from the number cubes. Here it may be helpful to use colors. By comparing the answer for problem 18 with that for 19d, you can call students' attention to the difference between theoretical and experimental chance, as explored in Section C.

21. Chances can be calculated by comparing the number of favorable outcomes to all possible outcomes.

22. Since there are three ways of getting a 10, there are 33 ways of not getting a 10. So there is a 33 out of 36 chance of not getting a 10. Similarly, since there are six ways of getting a 7, there are 30 ways of not getting a 7. So there is a 30 out of 36 chance of not getting a 7.

D Let Me Count the Ways

Notes

23b Suggest that students make a tree diagram to help see all the possible outcomes.

Treasure

During a hike along the shoreline at low tide, Hillary and Robert find a big chessboard on the sand.

On a nearby rock, they find this inscription:

Start in the lower left, Matey,
And toss a coin four times;
If ye have come to get the treasure here,
Then follow these instructions o' mine;
Go north with heads
And east with tails;
Dig in the place ye find;
Unless ye dig where most end up,
Ye won't have cents of mine!

23. Hillary and Robert could have tossed the coin four times and gotten HHHT.

    a. What route fits this result? On which square would they end?

    b. Other routes lead to the same square. How many different outcomes would lead to this square? Explain your reasoning.

24. Hillary and Robert toss the coin four times and follow the instructions from the inscription. Color all possible squares on the chessboard where they could end.

25. **Reflect** Hillary and Robert have time to dig only one hole before the tide comes back. Where will you tell them to dig for the treasure? Explain how you decide where to dig the hole.

Assessment Pyramid

25

Model real-life situations involving probability.

Reaching All Learners

English Language Learners

The poem contains some unusual wording. Have ELL students write the directions in a clearer way before they begin the problem.

Accommodation

Have students do only one path at a time and then repeat four times.

Solutions and Samples

23. a. The route is NNNE. They would end at a white square as shown:

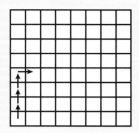

b. There are three other routes that lead to this square. If you replace H for heads by N for North and T for tails by E for East, the routes can be described by:

ENNN; NENN: NNEN

24.

EEEE

EENN

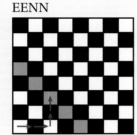

NNNN

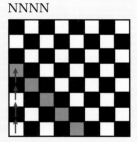

EEEN

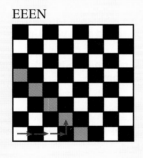

ENNN

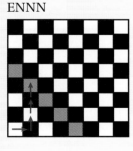

25. Answers will vary. Hillary and Robert should dig their hole at the square found by going two North and two East because these outcomes are more likely to occur than one North and three East or four North.

Hints and Comments

Materials

copies of the chessboard on page 31 of the Student Book, optional (one per pair or group of students)

Overview

Students help Hillary and Robert plan a route to dig for buried treasure on a large chessboard. Students first read a riddle that instructs them to:

- begin the game in the square in the lower left-hand corner of the chessboard,
- throw a coin four times, traveling north if the coin lands on heads and east if the coin lands on tails, and
- dig in the final location.

The four coin tosses must be one of the possible outcomes that occurs when tossing four coins. Each outcome leads to a square. Some outcomes lead to the same square.

About the Mathematics

Since each toss can be a head or a tail, there are $2 \times 2 \times 2 \times 2 = 16$ outcomes when tossing a coin four times. These 16 outcomes lead to five different squares. Six of the 16 outcomes will result in two heads and two tails: HHTT, HTHT, HTTH, TTHH, THTH, and THHT. This is the most likely outcome. Therefore, most students will tell Hillary and Robert to dig at a spot that is located two squares east and two squares north from the starting point.

Planning

You may want to make copies of the chessboard for each pair or group of students so that they can draw on it if they wish. You might also bring in a real chessboard and coins so that students can model the activity.

Comments About the Solutions

23. Students must find a way to "name" the square where this route ends. They can use directions in their answer.

25. A tree diagram is probably the easiest way to see that two heads and two tails are the most likely outcomes. Students may also draw paths on copies of the chessboard; the square with the most paths to it is the place in which to dig.

Notes

After having a student read the summary aloud, you may wish to have them go back through the section and find problems that support the concepts taught. This will encourage students to actively use the summary section as a study tool.

Be sure to discuss Check Your Work with your students so they understand when to give themselves credit for an answer that is different from the one at the back of the book.

Let Me Count the Ways

In this section, you learned that counting the number of ways an event can occur can help you find the chances of the event.

You can write all of the possible ways something can occur, or you can draw pictures. Tree diagrams are one type of helpful picture.

A tree diagram can give information about:

- all possible outcomes; and
- the chance any single outcome will occur.

Check Your Work

Here is a tree diagram of problem 3 (Robert's clothes) from page 27.

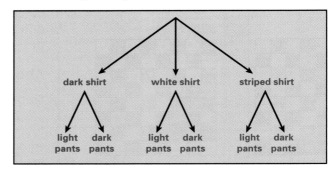

1. If Robert picks his clothes at random, what is the chance he will pick a striped shirt and light pants?

2. Draw a tree diagram that ends with eight branches. Write a story that fits your diagram.

Assessment Pyramid

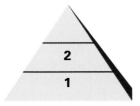

Assesses Section D Goals

Reaching All Learners

Parent Involvement

This final Summary offers an opportunity for parents to review the unit with their child.

Solutions and Samples

Answers to Check Your Work

1. The chance is $\frac{1}{6}$ or one out of six.

2. Show your story to a classmate to see if he or she agrees with your work. You may have different stories that start with different numbers of outcomes but be sure that your diagram ends in eight branches.

Hints and Comments

Overview

After reading the Summary, which reviews the main topics covered in this section, students solve problems about chance and tree diagrams. In Check Your Work students assess themselves on the concepts and skills from this section. Students can check their answers on page 40 of the *Take a Chance* Student Book.

Planning

After students complete Section B, you may assign for homework appropriate activities from the Additional Practice section, located on pages 34–36 of the *Take a Chance* Student Book.

Comments About the Solutions

1. Allow students to express their answers in different ways.

2. If this problem is too abstract for students, you can refer them to the tree diagram made for the families with two children. They may also look through the section to find other examples.

Extension

You can ask other questions using the tree diagram of Robert's clothes. You can also have students add additional clothing items to the tree diagram and formulate and answer their own questions.

D Let Me Count the Ways

Notes

For Further Reflection
Reflective questions are meant to summarize and discuss important concepts.

3. Robert has to choose his meal in a restaurant. For an appetizer, he can choose soup or salad. For the main course, he can choose vegetarian, fish, or beef. The desserts are ice cream and fruit salad. Make a tree diagram and count all of the possible three-course meals.

4. Robert and Hillary want to make a secret language with dots and dashes (· and –). They decide every letter of the alphabet should be an arrangement of four signs (dots or dashes). For instance, A will be ···· (4 dots), and B will be ··· – (dot, dot, dot, dash). Do they have enough combinations to make their secret language? You may use a tree diagram.

5. Invent a chance game that is not fair. Explain why it is not fair.

 For Further Reflection

Tree diagrams are very useful for solving certain types of problems. Describe when you might use a tree diagram. Give at least one problem as an example.

Assessment Pyramid

4, 5

3

Assesses Section D Goals

Reaching All Learners

Project

Have students make a board game that involves chance and tools used in this unit. They can play the game in class or you may use it for a parent night activity.

You may ask extra questions like: *How many of the three-course meals have soup? How many do not have fish?* You may also have students ask their own questions and answer them.

Solutions and Samples

3. The tree diagram can help you count.

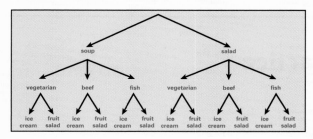

You may also reason that there are 2 × 3 × 2 = 12 possibilities.

4. No, there are only 16 possibilities. For each of the four positions in each combination of signs, you can use either a dot or a bar. So there are 2 × 2 × 2 × 2 = 16 different arrangements possible, but there are 26 letters in the alphabet. If arrangements with only 1, 2, or 3 signs were also allowed, there would be enough to make all 26 letters. This is how it is in Morse code.

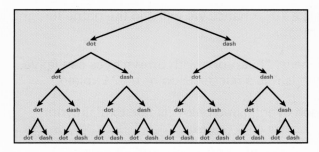

5. There are many possibilities. You can, for instance, make spinners with unequal parts. Discuss with a classmate whether your game is unfair.

For Further Reflection

Reflective questions are meant to summarize and discuss important concepts.

Answers will vary. Students should find and describe a problem where choices are or can be made; for example, the number of boys and girls in a family, the choice that can be made for different outfits, or the choices that can be made in a restaurant.

Hints and Comments

Comments About the Solutions

3. Some students may not need a tree diagram to find all possible combinations.

Extension

You can ask extra questions like: *How many of the three-course meals have soup? How many do not have fish?* You may also have students ask their own questions and answer them.

4. A tree diagram is very helpful when solving this problem, but students may need help setting it up.

5. If students need help, they may look through the unit and get ideas about different types of games.

Additional Practice

Section A Fair

1. In your own words, define each of the following.

   a. chance   **b.** fair

2. Give an example that shows how a coin could be used to do the following.

   a. make a fair decision

   b. make an unfair decision

3. Troy says, "There is a 70% chance we will win the game tonight." Explain what this means.

4. The teacher announces, "Everyone with brown eyes can leave school early today!" Is this a fair decision or not? Explain.

5. Decide whether each event listed below is fair. Explain your decision.

   a. All boys get five pieces of candy each, and all girls get four.

   b. All students with brown hair get an A.

   c. A bag is filled with 10 white marbles and 10 red ones. Without looking, you reach in the bag and grab a marble. If you grab a white one, your team goes first in the game.

   d. A bag is filled with 20 white marbles and 10 green ones. Without looking, you reach in the bag and grab a marble. If you grab a green one, your team goes first in the game.

Section B What's the Chance

1. Draw a ladder like the one on the left. Then put these statements about chance on the ladder.

   a. It will definitely happen.

   b. There is a 25% chance it will happen.

   c. It will not happen.

   d. There is a 0% chance it will happen.

   e. There is a 100% chance it will happen.

Section A. Fair.

1. a. Answers will vary. Refer to the Glossary on page 00 of this Teacher's Guide.

   b. Answers will vary. Refer to the Glossary on page 00 of this Teacher's Guide.

2.   Answers will vary. Sample responses:

   a. Two teams are playing against each other in a soccer game. They flip a quarter to decide which team gets the ball first.

   b. You say to your friend, "Let's flip a coin to decide who goes first. Heads, I win, and tails, you lose."

3.   Explanations will vary. The statement means that Troy thinks it is more likely than not she and her team will win the game.

4.   No, this is not a fair decision. It favors students with brown eyes.

5. a. Not fair. Boys get more pieces of candy than girls.

   b. Not fair. Getting an A should not depend on the color of your hair. Or, brown-haired students are favored.

   c. Fair. Each color, white or red, has an equal chance to come up.

   d. Not fair. The other team has twice as much chance to go first since there are twice as many white marbles as green marbles. It is much more likely that you will grab a white marble than a green one.

Section B. What's the Chance?

1.

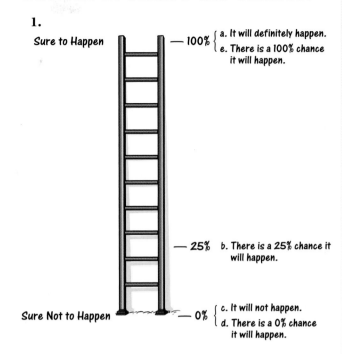

Sure to Happen — 100% { a. It will definitely happen. e. There is a 100% chance it will happen.

— 25% b. There is a 25% chance it will happen.

Sure Not to Happen — 0% { c. It will not happen. d. There is a 0% chance it will happen.

2. What number could you use to represent an event that is sure to happen?

3. What number could you use to represent an event that definitely will not happen?

4. What fraction could you use to represent each of the following chances?

    a. a 50% chance

    b. a 25% chance

    c. a 75% chance

5. a. Draw a spinner that can be used to make a fair decision.

    b. Explain why the spinner you drew in part **a** can be used to make a fair decision.

6. Put each of the following percents on a chance ladder.

    a. 10%   **d.** 75%

    b. 25%   **e.** 100%

    c. 50%

Section ◆ Let the Good Times Roll

1. In 100 coin tosses, about how many times would you expect heads to come up? Explain.

2. In 36 rolls of a number cube, about how many times would you expect to roll a 6?

3. a. Roll a number cube 36 times and record the results of each roll.

    b. How many times did you roll a 6?

    c. Compare your results for problem 3a with the predictions you made for problem 2.

    d. Compare your results for problem 3a with those of at least two other classmates. Did you get the same results? Is this reasonable or not?

Section B. (continued)

2.   1 or 100%

3.   0 or 0%

4. a. $\frac{50}{100}$ or $\frac{1}{2}$

 b. $\frac{25}{100}$ or $\frac{1}{4}$

 c. $\frac{75}{100}$ or $\frac{3}{4}$

5. a.   Drawings will vary. Sample drawing:

 b.   Explanations will vary, but should indicate why the drawing in problem 5a represents a fair spinner. Sample explanation:

The spinner is half green and half purple. So when you spin it, you can expect it to stop on purple half of the time and on green the other half.

6.

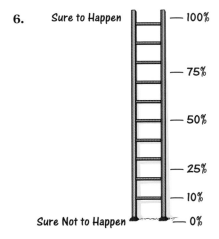

Section C.
Let the Good Times Roll

1.   If the coin is fair, it should land on heads half of the time and on tails the other half, or around 50 times each.

2.   six times

3. a.   Results will vary. Sample results:

Number Rolled	Number of Times It Came Up
1	✝✝✝
2	✝✝✝ ‖
3	✝✝✝ ‖
4	‖‖
5	✝✝✝ ‖‖‖
6	✝✝✝

 b.   Results will vary.

 c.   Answers will vary.

 d.   Answers will vary. Students should explain variations in their results.

Additional Practice

4. If you roll a number cube three times and get a 3 every time, what is the chance of getting a 3 on the next roll?

5. If you win the lottery once, will the first win improve your chances of winning again? Explain.

Section **D** Let Me Count the Ways

1. In your own words, explain what a tree diagram is and how it can be used.

2. If you have three shirts and three pairs of pants, how many different outfits can you make? Support your answer with a diagram.

3. If you roll two number cubes, what is the chance of rolling each of the following?

    a. doubles

    b. two even numbers

    c. two odd numbers

    d. two numbers that add up to 6

    e. two numbers that add up to 8

4. Suppose you have a bag of jellybeans that contains:

    10 red jellybeans
    20 green jellybeans
    15 yellow jellybeans
     5 purple jellybeans

    a. If you pull one jellybean out of the bag without looking, what color jellybean will you expect to get? Why?

    b. If you pull a jellybean out of the bag without looking, what is your chance of getting a purple one? Explain how you found your answer.

5. Make up a problem in which the chance of one outcome is twice as great as the chance of the other.

Section C. (continued)

4. 1 out of 6. Each roll of the number cube is independent of the roll before it.

5. No. Each lottery drawing is independent of other lottery drawings. Therefore, if you were to win one drawing, this would not affect your chances of winning another.

Section D.
Let Me Count the Ways

1. Answers will vary. Refer to the Glossary on page 00 in this Teacher's Guide.

2. There are nine possible outfits.

Sample diagram:

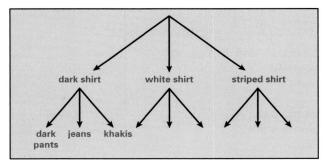

3. a. 6 out of 36, or $\frac{1}{6}$

   b. 9 out of 36, or $\frac{9}{36} = \frac{1}{4}$

   c. 9 out of 36, or $\frac{9}{36} = \frac{1}{4}$

   d. 5 out of 36, or $\frac{5}{36}$

   e. 5 out of 36, or $\frac{5}{36}$

4. a. Answers will vary. Sample response:

Since there are more green jelly beans than any other color, I would expect to get a green jelly bean.

   b. 5 out of 50, $\frac{5}{50}$ or $\frac{1}{10}$ or 10%.

Explanations will vary. Sample explanation:

There are five purple beans in a total of 50 beans. Each bean has the same chance to show up.

5. Problems will vary. Check that the two outcomes are $\frac{2}{3}$ and $\frac{1}{3}$.

Assessment Overview

Unit assessments in *Mathematics in Context* include two quizzes and a unit test. Quiz 1 is to be used anytime after students have completed Section B. Quiz 2 can be used after students have completed Section D. The unit test addresses most of the major goals of the unit. You can evaluate student responses to these assessments to determine what each student knows about chance and probability, and the strategies they use to solve each problem.

Pacing

Each quiz is designed to take approximately 25 minutes to complete. The unit test was designed to be completed during a 45-minute class period. For more information on how to use these assessments, see the Planning Assessment section on the next page.

Goals	Assessment Opportunities	Problem Levels
• understand the meaning of *fair* and how it relates to chance	Quiz 1 Problem 1a Test Problems 1 and 8	Level I
• know how to use tools for making fair decisions	Quiz 1 Problems 1b and 2ab Quiz 2 Problem 4b Test Problem 3	
• estimate and order chance events	Quiz 1 Problems 3abc and 4 Test Problems 4 and 5	
• express chance in percents, fractions, or ratios	Quiz 1 Problems 3abc and 4 Quiz 2 Problems 1a and 4a Test Problems 2, 4, and 7ac	
• list the possible outcomes of simple chance and counting situations	Quiz 2 Problems 2 and 3bc Test Problem 1	
• understand the meaning of *chance* or probability	Quiz 2 Problem 1b Test Problem 6	Level II
• use visual models to represent simple one-, two-, and three-event situations	Quiz 2 Problems 2 and 3abc	
• understand that variability is inherent in any probability situation	Quiz 2 Problem 1b Test Problems 7b and 8	Level III

About the Mathematics

These assessment activities evaluate the major goals of the *Take a Chance* unit. Refer to the Goals and Assessment Opportunities section on the previous page for information regarding the goals that are assessed in each problem. Some problems do not ask students to use a specific strategy (e.g., express chance as a fraction, a ratio, a percent, or in words). Students have the option of using strategies or representations with which they are comfortable. They may also use any of the models that are introduced and developed in this unit (tree diagrams, chance ladders, or a circular model like the spinner). Students are not expected to use any formal algorithms to solve these problems. Students should demonstrate understanding but not mastery of dealing with chance and probability.

Planning Assessment

If you want to evaluate each student's understanding and abilities, you may have students work on these assessment problems individually, or you may have the students complete the first five problems in pairs or in small groups and do the sixth problem individually. Make sure you allow enough time for students to complete the problems. Students are free to solve the problems in their own ways. They may use any of the models to solve problems that do not ask for a specific model.

Scoring

Solution and scoring guides are included for the each quiz and unit test. Suggested score points are provided for each problem. Partial credit should be provided when appropriate. In scoring the assessment problems, the emphasis should be on the strategies students use to respond to problems. The strategy a student chooses may indicate how well he/she understands the concepts of chance and probability. For example, a concrete strategy supported by drawings may indicate the connections a student has made between different mathematical representations more than an abstract, computational answer. Consider how well the students' strategies address the problem as well as how successful the students are at applying their strategies in the problem- solving process.

Use additional paper as needed.

Hillary and Robert use a color cube to decide who may play a
computer game during lunch. The color cube has six faces,
each a different color.

1. a. Robert says,"If red turns up, I will play, and if red does
not turn up you may play."

Is this fair? Explain why or why not.

b. Describe a fair way to decide, using the color cube, who
may play the game during lunch.

2. The next day, three students want to play the computer
game during lunch.

a. Can they use this spinner to decide
who may play in a fair way?

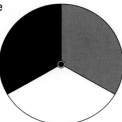

b. How would you change the spinner if six students want to
decide who may play the computer game?

3.   Use an arrow next to the chance ladder to place each event in the right place. For each event, write the chance as a fraction or as a percent.

a. A frog lands on a black square on the floor.

b. A coin is tossed and lands "heads."

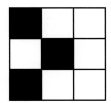

c. Hillary throws 5 with her number cube.

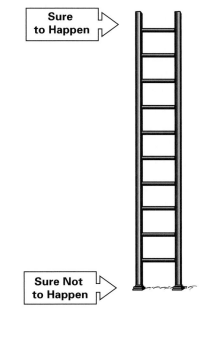

Sure to Happen ⇨

Sure Not to Happen ⇨

4. Match each event with its mathematical representation.

Story

a. My friend is going to raffle off a prize at a party. He makes 15 tickets and gives me three. What is my chance of winning the prize?

———

b. I am playing a game. If I throw 3 or 5 with a number cube, I will win. Is it likely that I will win? What is my chance?

———

c. Sam is thinking of a number greater than ten and less than 20. Ten and 20 are not allowed. What is my chance of guessing his number?

———

Statement

1. The chances are 1 out of 3 or $\frac{1}{3}$.

2. The chance is 0%.

3. There is an 80% chance.

4. There is a 50-50 chance.

5. The chance is $\frac{1}{9}$.

6. There is a 20% chance.

7. This is sure to happen.

Use additional paper as needed.

1.   Susan tosses a coin 50 times.
     a. How many "heads" are likely? Why?

     b. Is it possible for Susan to get 40 tails? Explain.

2.   Katrina is choosing an outfit to wear. Describe how many combinations she can make if she has four different blouses and three different pairs of slacks to choose from.

3.   Here you see a tree diagram representing the possibilities for a family with three children.
     a. In your tree diagram, circle the possibility where the first child is a girl, the second child is a boy, and the third child is also a boy.
     b. You can write the possibility, girl–boy–boy, as GBB for short.

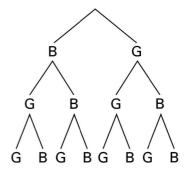

B = Boy
G = Girl

     Write down two other possibilities.

c. How many different possibilities are there in total for a family with three children?

d. What is the chance a family with three children has three boys?

4. Paula and Huong drew a sidewalk game for two players. They will use a spinner to decide how many steps to use.

Paula and Huong made these rules for the game:
- Move J: Go one step forward.
- Move K: Go two steps forward.
- Move L: Go three steps backward.
- Move M: Go back to START.

This is how they plan to make their spinner. There must be a chance of $\frac{1}{2}$ for move J, a chance of $\frac{1}{4}$ for move K, and the rest of the spinner must be divided in two equal parts for moves L and M.

a. Express the chances for moves L and M as a fraction.

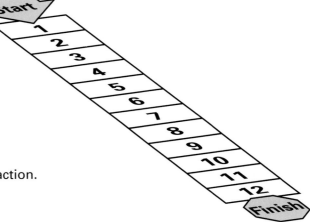

b. Design a spinner that fits the rules Paula and Huong made.

Use additional paper as needed.

1. **Choose <u>one</u> of the statements and in a few sentences explain what it means. You may use examples if you want to.**

   • Hillary and Robert want to make a *fair* decision about who may play the game.

   • There is a 25% *chance* frog Newton landed on a black tile.

   • A *tree diagram* gives information about all possible outcomes.

The director of the program tells the weatherman not to use "10% chance" in his talk.

2. **What should the weatherman say? Use words like *sure, very, not, almost,* and *likely*.**

Katrina is a student in a small school that has only six classes. Two classes at her school are invited to visit a television studio in a nearby city. The principal wants to use a fair method to select which two classes will go.

3. **Describe a fair method the principal can use to make the choice. Why do you think your method is fair?**

In the television studio, four of the students will be chosen to be on camera, two boys and two girls. Mr. Harris's class has 23 students, 8 boys and 15 girls. Ms. Lyne's class has 27 students, 12 boys and 15 girls.

4. **Katrina is in Ms. Lyne's class. She wonders how good her chances are for being chosen. Write her a note describing her chances.**

5. **Copy this chance ladder. Use arrows with a, b, c, and so on to mark the following events on the chance ladder:**

   a. **Tomorrow the sun will rise.**

   b. **There is a 50-50 chance that I will be able to visit you tonight.**

   c. **A bag is filled with 30 marbles, 20 are red and 10 are blue. If I take a marble out of the bag without looking, the chance I took a blue one is 1 out of 3.**

   d. **There is a 90% chance our team will win the game today.**

6. **Make up a chance-story for which this spinner can be used.**

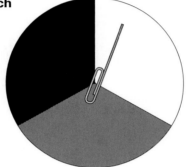

Have you ever seen a "Wheel of Fortune" at a fair? It is a big wheel with numbers along the edge. You may buy as many tickets as you want, and when all tickets are sold, the wheel is turned so fast that you cannot know which number it will show when it stops. If the number on your ticket shows up, you will win the prize.

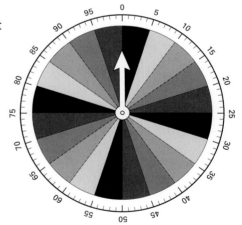

7. a. **Suppose you bought only one ticket. What is your chance to win the prize?**

   b. **How many tickets do you need to buy so that you can be sure to win the prize?**

   c. **Niles bought as many tickets as his age. He is 15 years old. Express the chance he has of winning the prize as a fraction and as a percent.**

8. **Belinda found an old coin. She tossed the coin, and heads came up on the first three tosses. Belinda said, "This coin is not fair anymore. It has worn off more on one side." Comment on Belinda's statement.**

Possible student answer	Suggested number of score points	Problem level
1. a. This is not fair. Each face of the color cube has the same chance of coming up and he has only one color.	1	I
b. Hillary and Robert can each choose a color. They are not allowed to choose the same color. Whose color comes up may play the game. If none of the chosen colors comes up, they throw again. OR Hillary and Robert each choose three colors. They are not allowed to choose the same colors. Whose color comes up may play the game.	2	I
2. a. Yes, they can use the spinner. Each student has the same chance of playing the computer game.	2	I
b. Possible student answers: • Divide the spinner in six equal parts by halving each current part. • Students make a drawing to show a division in six equal parts.	3	I
Check whether the statements are indicated in the right place on the chance ladder. **3. a.** 3 out of 9, which equals $\frac{1}{3}$ or about 30%. **b.** 50% or $\frac{1}{2}$ **c.** $\frac{1}{6}$ or a little less than 20%	9 (1 for each correct fraction and percent and 1 for a correct chance ladder)	I
4. a. statement 6 (3 out of 15 or $\frac{3}{15} = \frac{1}{5}$)	3 (1 for each correct match)	I
b. statement 1 (2 out of 6 or $\frac{2}{6} = \frac{1}{3}$)		I
c. statement 5 (1 out of 9 or $\frac{1}{9}$)		I
Total number of score points	20	

Possible student answer	Suggested number of score points	Problem level
1. a. I expect heads to come up 25 times, because heads and tails have an equal chance to occur.	**3** (1 point for the answer, 2 for a correct explanation)	I
b. That is possible. Only when you toss the coin a very large number of times can Susan expect the numbers of heads and tails to be equal.	**3** (1 point for the answer, 2 for a correct explanation)	II
2. There are 12 combinations.	**3**	II
3. a. Students should mark GBB in the tree diagram.	1	II
b. Students should mention two possibilities, chosen from: GGG; GGB; GBG; BGG: BGB; BBG; and BBB.	2	II
c. There are eight possibilities in total.	1	II
d. 1 out of 8 or $\frac{1}{8}$ or 12.5%	1	I
4. a. For moves L and M together there is $\frac{1}{4}$ available and the chances are equal, so $\frac{1}{8}$ each. OR Add the chances for moves J and K : $\frac{1}{2} + \frac{1}{4} = \frac{3}{4}$. For moves L and M there is $\frac{1}{4}$ available and the chances are equal, so half of $\frac{1}{4}$ or $\frac{1}{8}$ each.	**3** (2 points for the correct fractions and 1 for a correct explanation)	I
b.	**3** (The spinner should be neatly drawn and the sectors should match the fractions)	I
Total number of score points	**20**	

Possible student answer	Suggested number of score points	Problem level

1. Students should explain one of the three statements.
 	
  • The decision is *fair* if Hillary and Robert have equal chances to play the game.
 	
  • For every four tiles on the floor, one is black and three are white.
 	
  • The above example of a tree diagram shows possibilities for a family with two children. Possibilities are: GG; GB; BG; BB. You can see that the chance for two boys is 1 out of four or $\frac{1}{4}$ or 25%.
	2	I

2. Sample responses:
 	
  • It is very unlikely that it will be dry all day today.
 	
  • It is almost sure that it will <u>not</u> be dry all day today.
 	
  • It is not very likely that it will be dry all day today.
	2	I

3.   • Put one number that represents each class in a bag and draw twice from the bag.
 	
  • Using one number cube, assign one number to each class in the school. Roll the number cube twice. If the same number comes up twice, roll the number cube a third time.
 	
  • Using two number cubes, assign one number to each class in the school. Roll the number cubes once. If a double number is thrown, the roll does not count. Roll again.
 	
  • Make a spinner with six sections of equal size and spin it twice. If the same class is chosen again, spin a third time.
 	
  • Write all 15 combinations of two classes on individual cards. Put all the cards in a bag and choose one card.
 	
These methods are fair because each of the six classrooms has the same chance of being chosen.
	2	I

Possible student answer	Suggested number of score points	Problem level
4. • Divide the boys and girls into two separate groups. Using this method, Katrina (and any other girl) would have a 2 out of 30 chance of being chosen. • Choose one boy and one girl from each class. If this method is used, Katrina will have a 1 out of 15 chance of being selected.	3	I
5. a. 100% chance **b.** 50% chance **c.** 33% chance (Accept if arrow shows about 30%.) **d.** 90% chance	4	I
6. Accept any story in which each of three events (or each of three choices) or a similar division like two out of six has an equal chance to occur.	3	II
7. a. $\frac{1}{100}$ or 1%. **b.** 100 tickets **c.** $\frac{15}{100}$ or $\frac{3}{20}$; 15%	1 1 2	I III I
8. Belinda cannot be sure after only three tosses. Even with a new coin you could have three heads in a row.	2	III
Total number of score points	22	

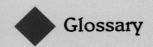
Glossary

The glossary defines all vocabulary words listed on the Section Opener pages. It includes the mathematical terms that may be new to students, as well as words having to do with the contexts introduced in the unit. (Note: The Student Book has no Glossary. Instead, students are encouraged to construct their own definitions, based on their personal experiences with the unit activities.)

The definitions below are specific for the use of the terms in this unit.

chance (p. 1) the possibility that an event will occur

experimental chance (TG p. 1A) the chance that an event occurred after an experiment was carried out

theoretical chance (TG p. 1B) the chance that an event may be expected to occur

fair (p. 2) giving equal chances to all possible outcomes

tree diagram (p. 3) a picture with branches representing all possible choices or combinations of choice

trial (p. 24) one of many repetitions of an experiment

BRITANNICA

Mathematics
in
Context

Blackline
Masters

Dear Family,

Very soon your child will begin the *Mathematics in Context* unit *Take a Chance*. The letter to your child below introduces and describes the unit and its goals.

You can help your child relate the classwork to his or her own life by asking for help in making fair decisions at home, such as choosing family members to set the table, empty the dishwasher, or clean a room.

Look for opportunities to bring chance and probability into the home. Discuss situations involving chance: the weather report or getting tickets for a special concert.

Have your child count the possible arrangements of the family members around the dinner table or at a movie theater. Talk about how likely it is that any two people will sit next to each other. If you have games that use number cubes or spinners, discuss how chance is involved in each game. Do the games seem to be fair? Check newspapers for statements about chance and read them to your child.

Chance is an important concept in dealing with uncertainty and is a factor in many situations, such as determining insurance rates, making predictions, and studying risk.

Enjoy helping your child begin to explore chance.

Sincerely,

The Mathematics in Context Development Team

Dear Student,

You are about to begin the study of the *Mathematics in Context* unit *Take a Chance*. Think about the following words and what they mean to you: *fair, sure, uncertain, unlikely,* and *impossible*. In this unit, you will see how these words are used in mathematics.

You will toss coins and roll number cubes and record the outcomes. Do you think you can predict how many times a coin will come up heads if you toss it a certain number of times? Is the chance of getting heads greater than the chance of getting tails? As you investigate these ideas, you are beginning the study of probability.

When several different things can happen, you will learn how to count all of the possibilities in a smart way. During the next few weeks, keep alert for statements about chance you may read or hear, such as "The chance of rain is 50%." You might even keep a record of such statements and bring them to share with the class.

We hope you enjoy learning about chance!

Sincerely,

The Mathematics in Context Development Team

Name _____

1. Put a check in the column that best describes your confidence that the event will take place.

Statement	Sure It Won't	Not Sure	Sure It Will
A You will have a test in math sometime this year.			
B It will rain in your town sometime in the next four days.			
C The number of students in your class who can roll their tongues will equal the number of students who cannot.			
D You will roll a 7 with a normal number cube.			
E In a room of 367 people, two people will have the same birthday.			
F New Year's Day will come on the third Monday in January.			
G When you toss a coin once, heads will come up.			
H If you enter "2 + 2 =" on your calculator, the result will be 4.			

Name _____

10. a. Color the first floor so that Newton
will have a 50% chance of landing
on a black tile.

b. Mark the 50% chance on the
scale (ladder).

c. What is another way of saying:
"The chance is 50%?"

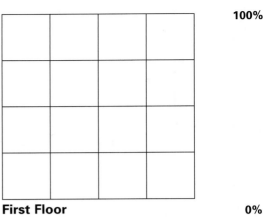

First Floor

100% —

0% —

12. a. Color the second floor so Newton's
chance of landing on a black tile
is 1 out of 5.

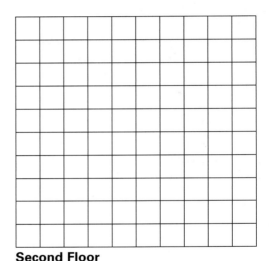

Second Floor

b. Color the third floor with any
pattern of black-and-white tiles.
What is the chance that Newton
will land on a black tile on the
floor you made?

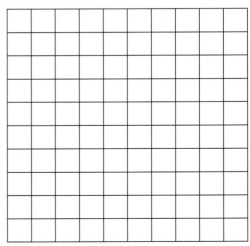

Third Floor

2. Connect all the statements that say the same thing.

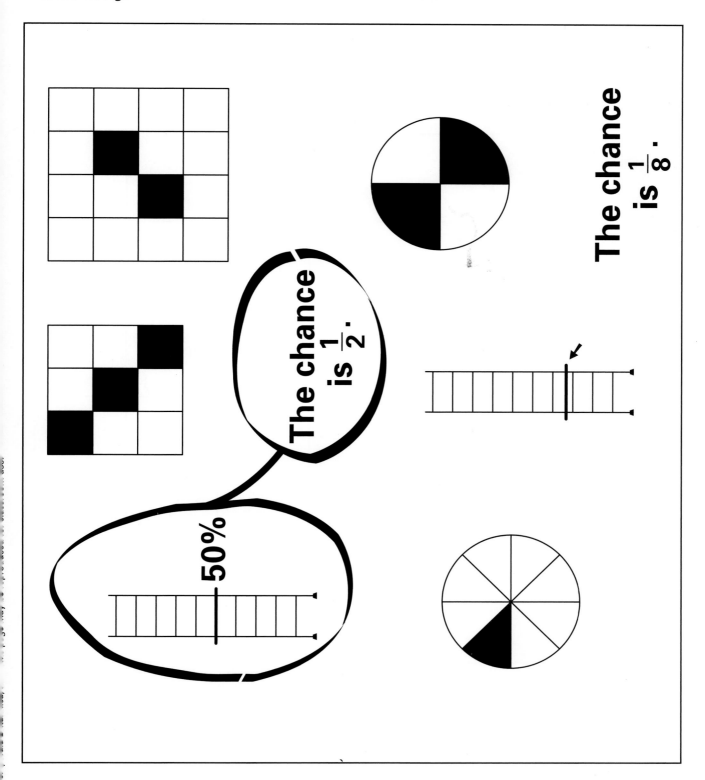

♦ **Student Activity Sheet 4**
Use with *Take a Chance*, page 30.

Name _____

19. a. For each square, fill in the sum of the numbers.

   b. How many different pairs are possible when you roll two number cubes?

   c. How many ways can you get a sum of 10 with two number cubes?

   d. What is the best number to pick if you are playing Sum It Up? Is your answer different from your choice in Problem 18?

6						
5						
4						
3						
2						
1						
	1	2	3	4	5	6